WHAT YOU DON'T
KNOW
IS HURTING YOU

WHAT YOU DON'T
KNOW
IS HURTING YOU

4 KEYS TO A PHENOMENAL CAREER

WITH NATHAN HALE WILLIAMS

MARION E. BROOKS

ISBN: 978-1-54393-703-9 (print)
ISBN 13: 978-1-54393-704-6 (ebook)

Editorial Services: Tanya Brockett, HallagenInk.com
Interior Design: **B**ookbaby
Cover Design: Trevor Ali, amaraREPS

Printed in the United States of America

For my grandparents, Elizabeth "Sunshine" Brooks
and Rev. A. A. Brooks:
I would not be able to do if they had not done for me!

TABLE OF CONTENTS

FOREWORD

By Sherlaender "Lani" Phillips, Microsoft Corporation

———————◆———————

When I first discovered this book, I thought, *Why didn't I have this when I started my career?*

After growing through the ranks in one of the most recognizable companies in the world, Microsoft Corporation, I have come to know the immense value of this book you hold in your hands. *What You Don't Know* IS *Hurting You: 4 Keys to a Phenomenal Career* truly lays out the blueprint for how to accelerate your career. Marion Brooks is spot on in selecting and outlining the Four Ps: Performance, Perceptions, Positioning, and Persistence. Understanding these elements and how they impact your career growth is essential if you desire to excel.

In my positions at Microsoft, I have had to work hard to earn each of my promotions. I started as an individual contributor in a technical position and transcended into a senior executive role, so I know it can be done. Thankfully, I understood the principles that Marion shares in this book. Marion shortens the learning curve for you and shortens your timeline because he is giving you the blueprint. This is true whether you are early career, mid-career, or in the last chapter of your career. This book has something for everyone.

As you work through the Four Ps in this book, pay close attention to the Performance discussion on Emotional Intelligence (EQ) and your Intelligence Quotient (IQ). I grew up in a culture where IQ was praised, yet I was more accelerated in EQ than most. This has served me well in my twenty-one years at Microsoft Corporation. In the corporation of the future, this is the skill that will be the differentiator. Yes, your IQ is important for establishing your position in an organization, but EQ is essential to career longevity and advancement. As Marion says, "A high IQ will get you hired, but a high EQ will get you promoted." This information opens the book as Chapter 1 because it is so critical to your career growth and the ability to be successful in the other three Ps. My career is testament that having a strong EQ is essential. Don't miss this.

The guidance provided in the area of Perceptions will help you to show up with confidence and alignment with how you want to be viewed by others. This will be important to you as you grow in your career because hiring decisions are often made when you are not in the room. How others perceive you at that time will drive decisions about your professional future. That perception is not only impacted by your appearance (package), body language, and confidence, but also by the personal story you share about your experience, accomplishments, and goals. Interviewers don't want to have to read the résumé and talk to fifty people to learn this; they want you to be able to represent what you have done and what you can bring to the company. Being able to articulate your value through your personal brand story with confidence (not arrogance) will make a powerful difference in how your personal brand is perceived and in how well you leverage it.

In the early stages of your career, you had to interview for positions and your focus was to prepare for that interview. As you move into the executive ranks, sponsorship becomes more critical. In the chapters on Positioning, Marion defines and reveals how to leverage mentors and identify sponsors. He clarifies the difference between the two and shows you how to develop those relationships. I agree that sponsorship is key to making transitions. Early in my career, I learned a great deal and wanted to perform well and do a good job, but working really hard and getting good results was not enough to accomplish the career goals I had in front of me. (That just brought in more work!) I then learned the value of relationships and was ultimately sponsored into positions that were in alignment with my career plans. I acknowledge that I had a ton of grace throughout my career, but developing and honoring mentor and sponsor relationships has allowed me to reach the heights I have enjoyed. Look at your internal and external network: do you have mentors and sponsors in place? Do you have a rich network you can go to for help in solving problems for your team? Whether yes or no, Section III of this book will help in this area.

The final of the Four Ps is Persistence. It is important that you build the skills, the muscles, and the resilience you need when you fall down so you know how to get back up. This book doesn't promise that everything will be easy and you will never have to face adversity. That is not a likely scenario. The examples in Chapter 9 show that it is not always easy rising to the top. You will have moments when you lose your self-awareness or you fail to see the opportunities in the obstacles. Recognize that you will need to continue learning on your career path. Resilience will help you to recover from failures along the way. Persistence will help you to see your career plan through.

Marion and I have more than career accolades and success on the executive level in common. We also share a bond of being the first generation in our families to succeed in Corporate America. We didn't have the benefit of sage advice from elders who have climbed to the top in large organizations. We had to learn, grow, and endure a few hard knocks in our journeys, but it is in the difficult times that you learn. We both had support from different sources along the way, such as great mentorship and sponsorship, but we still had to make the corporate climb without familial precedence. Thankfully, now that Marion has written this book, you won't have to make what could be a challenging climb alone.

This book will give you a framework to build on. The client examples will show you the impact of the principles in a corporate setting, and the exercises will help you to apply the learning and put it into practice for yourself. You will then be able to ask, "Did that really work for me or did it not?" And then you grow from your own honest answers. Don't hold yourself back. Use this blueprint to excel in your career. I have no doubt it will help you to dream bigger, go further, and better enjoy your corporate journey to success.

—Sherlaender "Lani" Phillips
Chief Transformation Officer,
Microsoft Corporation (2018)

PREFACE

By Nathan Hale Williams

I have known Marion Brooks for over a decade. That's not entirely true. I have known "Big" for a decade. I always wondered the origin of his nickname and I honestly didn't know that his real name was Marion until two years ago. (Marion is the same name as my late grandfather and uncle.) Over the course of co-writing this book, I was introduced to Marion E. Brooks and quickly understood why I can't stop calling him "Big."

Marion came to me for advice on writing a book based on his years of experience as an executive and an executive coach. After our informational meeting, Marion and I spoke more about this project and his mission in writing it. Ultimately, we both agreed that partnering on the project would be a great fit. When I agreed to co-write this book with him, I had no idea that I would be learning far more than I taught; that I would be receiving much more than I gave. It truly has been an enlightening, educational, and uplifting exercise for me from beginning to end.

In this age, there are countless people attempting to give us advice on television, in social media, and in person. Quite honestly, I always assess the adviser's own life to determine the credibility of the advice given. I can sincerely say that Marion walks the walk and epitomizes all of what he is teaching in this wonderful book. It's a book I wish I had when I was entering the workforce over twenty years ago. It is a book I will make sure my niece and nephew read before they do. It is a book that I know for sure will add value to your life professionally and personally.

I am so proud to be a part of this project. I am also proud to know a professional like Marion who practices what he preaches. And now, I can call him "Big" and mean it.

INTRODUCTION

---◆---

Throughout my career as an executive and an executive coach, I have enjoyed a variety of roles that have afforded me a bird's-eye view on how successful people move through corporate environments and their professional lives in general. One of the epiphanies I had early on is that high potentials, or people who are seen as such, are provided different information, training, support, and feedback than everyone else. Ultimately, success becomes a self-fulfilling prophecy whereby the people who are provided more information and opportunities seek and receive more information as well as opportunities. However, having access to the information does nothing if you're not willing to act upon the information. The most successful people have both—access and the action behind it. I have coached such clients who work for some of the best-known companies in the world including, JP Morgan Chase, HBO, and Capitol Records, as well as clients in medium, small, and start-up businesses.

Learning from my personal experiences and those of my clients' is my "why" for this book. My goal is to provide access to the insights and perspectives that only a chosen few usually receive. In Corporate America, the "chosen few" are called high potential achievers or "high potentials." According to the Harvard Business Review, on average, only five percent of employees will be identified as being high potential.

Unfortunately, if you are a woman, person of color—or other minority—that number is even lower. These high potentials receive advantages that the other ninety-five percent do not, including: support, guidance, personal development, insights, mentors, and so on.

The 1980s film *Trading Places* starring Eddie Murphy and Dan Aykroyd best illustrates my point regarding access for the five percent of high achievers versus the remaining ninety-five percent. In the film, a wealthy trust fund heir, Louis Winthorpe III (played by Aykroyd), and a homeless street hustler, Billy Ray Valentine (played by Murphy), become entangled in a social experiment and gambling bet staged by the Duke brothers, who are commodities brokers. The storyline is a contemporary take on the classic nineteenth century novel by Mark Twain, *The Prince and the Pauper*.

After witnessing Valentine and Winthorpe interact on the street, the Duke brothers debate whether it is nature versus nurture that determines our fate in life. They frame Winthorpe and free Valentine from jail, installing him in Winthorpe's former position at the brokerage. They give Valentine all the lessons in business, professional and social etiquette, and the other insights and training that a privileged person acquires (i.e., access) over the course of his life in order to test his ability to thrive. Valentine not only thrives, he surpasses their expectations.

Coupling his street smarts and his own natural ability with the new education, Valentine thrives based on the information received from the Dukes. Once they realize the experiment is over—and Valentine has succeeded—they exchange their "usual amount" bet of one dollar and decide to return each of the men back to their normal standings. The good news is that Valentine catches onto their scheme, and, ultimately, he works with Winthorpe to seek revenge on the Dukes.

Consider this book as your personal Duke brothers, except the goal is far more altruistic and my mission is to help you maximize and nurture your potential and impact. I'm also willing to bet more than one dollar that if you apply the lessons in this book, you will see results.

In addition to my credentials as an internationally certified executive coach and a corporate leader with over twenty years of experience in the pharmaceutical industry, I was also deemed a high potential very early in my career. I was given access that I will be sharing with you throughout the book.

Another goal of this book is to take you behind the curtain and share what I received as a high potential, plus what I have learned over my career leading, mentoring, and now coaching successful, high net worth people. I believe that nurture—through the various lessons we experience—is far more indicative of our success than those achieved through our nature. Some information will seem like common sense, but like my grandmother, Sunshine Brooks, used to say, "Common sense ain't common if it's not applied." Those lessons are designed to increase your self-awareness so that you can make better and more impactful choices. Other lessons and techniques will provide elevated insight into the ways in which highly successful people are trained and how they use that training to make better decisions. Use this book and the tools provided herein to effectuate your own version of *Trading Places*.

My personal story is the perfect example of how you can change your natural circumstances into something far greater than ever imagined with consistent nurturing. When I was born on the Southside of Fort Worth, Texas (sidebar: I recently met someone from Fort Worth at a business conference, and when I told them I was from the Southside, they were shocked), due to my family situation, I was not pegged as a future achiever. I wasn't supposed to make it out of the Southside of Fort Worth; if you made your assessment about my future based on the circumstances into which I was born. In fact, most people wrote me off from the beginning due to my family's dynamics.

None of the indicators for success were there. My parents weren't married and thus I was considered a bastard child to some people, even those in my own family. My mother has three children and we have three different fathers. She was the youngest child of four children born to a southern Baptist preacher and the first to have a child out of wedlock. Not to be outdone, my dad has eleven children by ten different women (my oldest brothers are twins), and some considered him a street thug. So, as you can see, this was not the typical recipe for a future corporate executive or executive coach. My maternal brother, sister, and I lived with my grandparents, who were on a tight, fixed income after raising their four children, some of my older cousins, and numerous others who were not related by blood.

Notwithstanding the reality of my youth, this is not a pity party. I turned out pretty well, but none of it would've been possible without the Sunshine in my life—my grandmother. Her full name was Elizabeth Sunshine Brooks. Actually, Sunshine was the birth name given to her by her half-Native American grandmother. Later, my grandmother would put Elizabeth in front of Sunshine (more than likely to make it easier for her to assimilate into the community). But, Sunshine was unavoidably sunshine personified, and so everyone knew her as Sunshine Brooks.

My grandmother was just like everything you think about and associate with the actual sunshine. She provided warmth, energy, peace, and nourishment—all of the things that motivate, inspire, and energize you to do your best. Had it not been for Sunshine and my grandfather, Reverend A.A. Brooks; my brother, sister, and I would have most likely ended up in the foster care system…or worse. Before I learned the word altruism, my grandmother was living the example of it daily. It was well known that the Brooks' home always had an open door waiting to support and mentor anyone—family or not.

The lessons I learned about service to others would become the precursor and backbone to my success over the years. I learned those early lessons from Sunshine, and she learned it from her grandmother who'd stepped in to raise her after her mother died in a freak accident. Her grandmother learned that Sunshine's stepfather was abusing her, so she took Sunshine in. And Sunshine's backbone was my grandfather, Reverend Brooks (as he was commonly called). Together, they provided me with a home and a foundation that would forever impact and change my life. I am their living legacy of sacrifice and service.

I remember watching my grandmother go about her day. After making breakfast and making sure we had what we needed for school, she went to work for the day. She would then come back and help everybody in our house; whoever happened to be there, and with whatever you happened to need. She was so selfless that often times I thought she was angelic. In contrast, when my mother visited, or when she temporarily lived with us, her volatile personality often disrupted the household harmony. She could be very mean and had many issues with my grandmother. I think she resented her on many levels, but it would be years before I realized why. We will explore what I learned from this dynamic in later chapters.

Now, I am focused on investing in you, giving you access, and helping you to understand why *What You Don't Know Is Hurting You* because my grandmother and so many other people invested in me and gave me access. I must admit; however, that I am not solely writing this book for you. This book and my coaching are helping me fulfill a legacy of giving and investing in others beginning (to my knowledge) with my great-great-grandmother to my grandmother and down to me. Everything provided in this book is my way of continuing my grandmother's and my great-great-grandmother's legacy of investing in others.

As I said, my grandparents didn't have a lot. We went through some really tough times. There was a time period when all we had to eat were potatoes and Party Time hot dogs, which were so cheap that they turned the water pink when you boiled them. We had to eat them for breakfast, lunch, and dinner. It forced us to get creative with food preparation. For breakfast, we fried the hot dogs. For lunch, we boiled them. For dinner, the dogs were baked. We did something different with the potatoes for each meal as well. Had those creative cooking shows been around then, my family and I would have surely been first in line at the auditions. The funny thing is, my sister and I hated those hot dogs so much we created a song about how awful they were (we still laugh about that song today).

When I was in high school, my grandmother's car broke down and we didn't have the money to get it fixed or get a new one. We were without a car for a few years, which was a big deal living in spread out Texas. Those were some tough times, but my grandparents always found a way to help others and never made us feel like a burden. The way they treated others, and me, taught me a lot about being benevolent and supportive to others. It also taught me how to manage what I have.

When I was about twelve, Sunshine started having me help her manage the household bills. She taught me how to set a budget and payment schedule, and she ultimately turned over that responsibility to me. She helped me open my first bank account at sixteen. She was really focused on ensuring that I understood financial management and the importance of education. She went to college, and although she didn't finish, it was a big deal for a black woman in her day to even finish high school let alone go to college. She used to say, "I was born in 1915 in Texas and I went to college as a black woman. You have no excuse not to go to college."

> ## "I was born in 1915 in Texas and I went to college as a black woman. You have no excuse not to go to college."
>
> —Mrs. Sunshine Brooks

Even with her encouragement, it was easier said than done for someone with my background.

One thing I will give my mother—both of my parents, actually—is that they encouraged and expected us to get good grades. Thankfully, I always earned good grades, as school was something that came easy for me. My mother is one of the smartest people I know—her IQ is off the charts—and she demanded that we work hard in school. When she was around and we got anything less than a B, we'd be punished with a large security guard belt. Getting a C gave us one lick; a D was three licks; and an F was, "Oh, you're getting f***ed up." You were screwed. My brother got a lot of Fs (he's going to kill me, but it's the truth). Jokes aside, everyone expected us to do our best. The thought was if you are doing your best, success is inevitable. If we needed help, then they empowered us to ask for it. Many of the subjects—like math—seemed very intuitive to me and didn't require me to study a lot. The more challenging classes were the ones I put in the extra work to get the grades I wanted because my family made sure I understood how important education was to my future.

However, it wasn't such a good thing for popularity in my neighborhood. There was a stigma that still exists today (especially in communities of color) that if you were smart and doing well in school then you were weak or soft, especially for young men. I don't know where that comes from—aside from residual effects of oppression. But, that's a different book. With that said, I took an entirely different approach. My response was always, "If you're dumb, you're weak, and you have no future." Naturally, I have learned better ways to debate an issue. That worked for that time and it separated me to a degree from some of the people I grew up around. My brother and my favorite cousin got caught up in the distractions and ended up facing a number of challenges in life. Instead, I was focused on what Sunshine had instilled in me about what she was able to do being born in 1915. She was right; I had no excuse.

As a result of doing so well in school, many people told me that I should go to college. But when I entered high school, I decided that after graduation I would land a job so that I could start earning money quickly. I was sick of being broke! Well thankfully, my mother had a plan to put me back on track. The summer after my freshman year of high school, my mother secured a job for me laying bricks. In Texas. In the summer. In the Texas Summer heat. I had to be there at 6:00 AM, and I finished when it was dark. It was hard, backbreaking work that I hated. At the end of the summer, I looked at the calluses on my hands and felt the ache in my back, and knew I would rather work hard with my brain than with my hands. I complained about the job to my mother. Her mission had been accomplished. "Well, that's the option if you don't want to go to college," she said. It was then and there I decided that I needed to wear a suit to work and not lay bricks in the hot Texas sun every day.

Even with my mother's great lesson, the biggest problem with college was my lack of resources. We had none and college was expensive. As I said, I was sick of being broke and the idea of going to college didn't seem feasible. I knew someone who had gone to a trade school, so I decided that was a good compromise (to avoid those bricks). Sunshine wasn't having any of it. "If that's what you want to do, I'm not going to fight you. But, I think there's more in you than that, think long-term not short-term," she said repeatedly.

My high school math teacher, Ms. Mitchell, also drove the point home that I needed to go to college. She sat me down one day and said, "You know, you have a bright future. You have to go to college because I believe you will be extremely successful in college and after you graduate. But you will limit yourself if you don't go. You are beyond and bigger than what you're thinking."

So, no trade school. No job. I was going to college.

Of course, I had no clue about how to get there and my high school counselor wasn't much help. Like I said, my grandmother went to college, but it was a different time by that point. She did find a program for students from low-income households that helped me through the process. I was assigned a counselor who assisted me with my applications, financial aid, and scholarships. Sunshine was with me every step of the way. My dad, mom, and Aunt Donnie were also super supportive. They all constantly encouraged me and told me how bright my future was. I know college isn't for everyone, but they helped me to believe that it was for me.

With the support of my family and some of my teachers, I was on the pathway to college. I just had to choose which college to attend. It was a big decision and because of my grades, I had options. My grandmother's brother (Uncle Dave) was an alum of a prestigious university halfway across the country and he made me an offer. He said if I went to his alma mater, he would pay for it.

I also visited a university closer to home because it had a "Top 10" accounting program, which was my intended major. I was really excited about the possibility of moving across the country and following in my great-uncle's footsteps. In the midst of making one of the biggest decisions in my life (at that time), I had to consider my family. My sister (who had been my best friend and chief advocate growing up) was now a single mom with an absentee father; I knew I couldn't go too far. Instead, I opted to stay close to home so I could be a father figure for my niece and help my sister raise her.

Even though I had decided to stay close to home, I knew I wanted the campus life experience, so I lived on campus my freshman year. The environment shell shocked my life. My high school was predominantly African American and Latino. My new university was predominantly white with huge class sizes of over one hundred students, and oftentimes, I was the only African American in the class. *Whoa!* It was a bit intimidating and stressful at first. I thought, *Do they know my background? Can they tell that I don't belong here?* I then decided that my goal was to represent my race in the best way I knew how—by succeeding. I put a great deal of pressure on myself—I felt that whatever I did or however I performed in these classes was a representation of all African Americans. I don't know if that is necessarily the strategy I would use now, but it worked for me then.

As you can imagine, it was a challenging school, particularly for people of color (POC). Amongst POC, the matriculation and graduation rates were extremely low. For that reason, I was committed to getting through and graduating, not only to defy those odds, but also because I had a plan for the life I wanted to live. More importantly, I wanted to ensure that my nieces and two younger cousins; Desmond and Joe, for all of whom I was the father figure in their lives, didn't have the same experiences that I had with finances and the other challenges I endured as a kid. I wanted to be their go-to resource. I wanted to make a difference in their lives like Sunshine had made in mine by supporting them and showing them what was possible.

My sister eventually had three more beautiful girls (one while I was in college and two more later in life) and I eventually had one of my own. Everyone who knows me, either personally or professionally, knows about my four girls: Morgan (my biological daughter) and my three nieces—Christarian, Montrese, and Hennette. I had to invest in all of my girls just like Sunshine had done for me, and her grandmother had done for her, to make sure that they were properly nurtured, told that success was possible, and given a chance to succeed.

During my first two years in college, I kept to myself and stayed under the radar. I didn't know a lot of people because I was constantly going home to help out around the house. Then tragedy struck my family. My two-year-old niece Mashaela died of a rare viral pneumonia. I was devastated. I was angry. And I was confused. I loved her so much! That was the darkest time of my life. I had never felt pain like that before and I wasn't sure I could recover. My sister was so strong during that time; to this day I don't know how she did it. I know inside she was dying. Through that tragedy, I learned two important lessons. First, life is short; second, not only was it important for me to do things for my family, I also had to do things for me.

I had always thought about pledging a fraternity, but put it off because I told myself that I was too busy and had too many responsibilities. After I finally regrouped from Mashaela's death, I decided a go to an interest meeting for Kappa Alpha Psi Fraternity, Inc.—a black Greek letter organization—and that changed everything. Uncle Dave was a Kappa, and I also felt they were the only choice for me. After I was initiated, I went from being in the shadows just doing my schoolwork to being a "big" man on campus. It was certainly a pivotal moment for me in college. Not only because of the typical social aspect of joining a fraternity (those parties are still legendary), but the leadership positions I would go on to hold. My tragedy had prompted me to take action that led me in a new direction (we will talk in later chapters about how adversity can lead us to new opportunities if we hang in there and put in the work).

During the semester after I pledged, I became the Polemarch (President) of our undergraduate chapter (Iota Alpha). Our chapter went from not having a lot of fanfare to being one of the premier chapters in the Southwest Province. As a result of the service, the other work we were doing, and the guidance and support of two brothers from the Arlington-Grand Prairie alumni chapter (Michael Glover and Wallace "Blinky" Williams), I was elected to the Province (regional) board of directors as the undergraduate over the entire state of Texas. It was following in Sunshine's footsteps of service to others that raised my visibility on campus and throughout the state. It was that *service* that helped me to finally step into my nickname. My first name is Marion, but most people call me, "Big." I was given that family nickname because I was such a chubby baby. Like really chubby. Okay, I was a fat baby; I'll admit it. However, as I grew older, the weight shed, but the name stuck. It became a central part of who I am and how I define my success both professionally and personally.

In college and beyond, service to others made me "Big." And I have the letterman jacket to prove it with "Big Time" across the back. Seriously, I can look back to that time and understand that it was really when I first began to apply the lessons I learned from my grandmother and when I set the foundation for the leader I would become. If you know anything about fraternities, or any organization for that matter, you know that you will find yourself leading people of various levels of commitment and skill. I had to use those tools that I saw exhibited at home to take our chapter and our fraternity to the next level. I learned that I had a lot of work to do to become more like Sunshine when dealing with conflict. I think some of my fraternity brothers would agree.

On the academic front, I was heading towards graduation. I switched my major from accounting to marketing. Accounting was not for me; I wanted to engage with people not spreadsheets. My plan was to build my career at an advertising agency and eventually start my own advertising company.

Throughout college, I had been working part-time with Ariel Nursing, which is a home health agency. The owner, Doris Carter, was a long-time family friend, neighbor, and mentor. She is my best friend Michael Baker's aunt, and I affectionately called her Aunt Doris. She offered me a full-time job at the agency after graduation that I accepted. It allowed me to do something I was familiar with while learning new skills and remaining close to my family. It was certainly a win-win to join the agency as its office manager. I graduated on Saturday and I started the new role on Monday.

Once I started at the agency full-time, Aunt Doris began to groom me in the various aspects of the business. She intended for me to take over the business once she retired. My role there was definitely integral to my acquisition of a broad set of management skills and training that I use to this day.

Once again, I had an example of how service to others was such a top factor when it came to effective management. Just like my grandmother, Aunt Doris had very high standards and expectations. She was a tough, but loving woman. If she saw you were trying, she would invest the time and effort to help you get better. The difference was that Aunt Doris began to teach me about making strategic business decisions. She also showed me that you get the best out of people when you demonstrate that their ideas and presence are important to you. Beyond that, she was very focused on the patients.

I remember so many instances that if a patient and their family couldn't afford to pay the fees, she wouldn't just walk away. Either she would do the caregiving work herself, or she would pay someone to do it out of her own pocket. I saw up close her passion for people, which correlated to the high level of success she was having based on her intention to be a vessel of support to others. I was also learning strategic thinking, executing with excellence, developing outcomes, problem solving, and never making excuses. It was an amazing start to my professional life within the comfort of a relationship that I'd had since I was a kid.

In the late nineties, the home health care business became extremely challenging due to the changes with Medicare during that time. Basically, the government was delaying Medicare payments, which impacted the bulk of our patients. I was in charge of billing, payroll, and benefits, so I knew the state of the books. Many times, we had hundreds of thousands of dollars that were outstanding from the government. It forced Aunt Doris to consider selling the business.

Just as Aunt Doris contemplated selling the business, a fraternity brother (Leonard Denton) called and suggested that I look into pharmaceutical sales. It was something completely foreign to me, but he encouraged me to go talk to a guy who was hiring. The only problem was that "the guy" already had a candidate in mind. I went to the meeting anyway so that I would at least have my name out there if I ultimately decided it was something I wanted to pursue. We met twice. After the second meeting, he changed his mind and offered me the position. He saw something special in me and thought I could bring value to the company. I was conflicted because I did not want to leave Aunt Doris, especially in a difficult time, so I asked her what I should do. She told me to take the opportunity because she was not certain what she was going to do with the company. So, I did. Six months later she sold the company.

When I started in pharmaceutical sales, I had a lot going on—to say the least. I was in graduate school. I was selling real estate on the weekends to pay for grad school. I was the Polemarch (president) of my fraternity's alumni chapter, and I held many other roles in the fraternity. In the midst of all of this, I became a father. When I first saw my daughter Morgan I instantly fell in love. I was amazed that I had helped create something so incredible. I was overjoyed, and at the same time overwhelmed and stressed out. I thought, *What if I'm a bad father? What if she doesn't like me?* I had been helping raise kids since I was fourteen, but now this one was mine and I was afraid of not being good enough for her. Now, there was definitely no room for failure or negative thoughts. I had to prioritize my plan for success and keep moving forward towards my goals. It's tiring to think about that time in my life, but somehow, I made it work.

My new career started off great. I won "Rookie of the Year" my first year in pharmaceutical sales and successfully launched a new product. Although I was getting a lot of attention in sales, I knew that I wanted to get back to management. Even with the success I enjoyed the first year, I still felt outside of my comfort zone. There were definitely moments when I doubted my ability to thrive in that environment with all the technical and medical terms that we were required to master. Plus, I was co-parenting my daughter with her mom. Every time it would get rough and I would get anxious, I would say to myself, "Someone has done this before, so I can too. Buckle up Big and get it done." It kept me focused and I began to get into the job. I realized that once again, my job was to serve people. I was there to serve the doctors, who in turn served their patients. Turning my focus back to service really energized the work and I became more comfortable doing the tasks of the job.

> Someone has done this before, so I can too!

As much as I was enjoying my job in sales, my eyes remained on getting back into management. Unfortunately, the company where I was working was going into a downturn with potential layoffs. There was no opportunity for me to advance into a management role. However, a competitor approached me about joining their team. I wanted to be loyal to the company where I was employed so I discussed the opportunity with my boss who advised that the prospects where I was were bleak and I should take the new position. I knew that I didn't want to take the new role unless there was a pathway to management, so I let the hiring manager know my intentions.

He assured me that if I did a good job and delivered high numbers that he would recommend me for the management development program. Within a year, my performance was good, and he kept his promise of recommending me for the program.

This proved to be a pivotal time in my career. I believe it was the first time within a company that senior level management identified me as a high potential achiever. I won the MVP award and successfully launched a new product. I went from Marion Brooks in Dallas, Texas, to receiving more exposure from a regional and national level. I flew to New Jersey to attend a three-week section of the management development program where I was responsible for a group of five new hires that I mentored throughout the orientation process. It was in those sessions that I was taught the various coaching techniques on how to motivate and manage employees effectively.

After I completed the management program, I had an opportunity to become a manager in Texas, but I was also being considered for a training role in New Jersey. Once again, my plans placed me at a crossroads and a potential pivot. I evaluated it from this perspective: I felt that I could go and be a good manager now; however, if I were able to spend the additional time in training—because I was always interested in training and teaching people—I would become an even better manager. Taking a full-time training role also afforded me the ability to network with people throughout the entire organization and to become a better resource for my team. Being in training wasn't even remotely close to what I had planned. I had my heart set on management. Ultimately, it was perfect for my advancement along the path toward a high-level management role.

I spent two years training new hires and learning more about effective coaching techniques, all the while networking throughout the organization. During that time, I won another high-profile award. I was the first skills trainer to win the Training Excellence Award. At this point, I was definitely on the high potential list, and I was getting access to many incredible mentors and champions (we'll talk more about the difference later in the book). I sought people out for mentorship. And people were seeking me out for mentorship. In fact, my next role was birthed out of a mentoring meeting.

I was in a meeting with one of my mentors, when he said, "This is turning into an interview. I have a position that I think you'd be great for and I want to talk to you about it." Another unexpected pivot. The next day I interviewed with his boss and the following month became an area sales manager for the New York region. For sure, it was after I started that role when I was pegged as high potential across the organization. But had I not taken a leap of faith and been flexible with my plans, I would never have been recognized. The pivot to the training department put me on a larger platform for senior management to see what I could do. Then, they were willing to invest in my career and me. I converted mentors into sponsors.

As an Area Sales Manager, more awards came like "Manager of the Year" as well as a number one designation in the entire country. I was accepted into the Leadership Discovery Program; so I was on my way, or at least I thought I was. During what we call a "360°Review" my manager told me that I wasn't always exhibiting executive presence. He clarified by saying, "You have all these great ideas. You have all these amazing things you're doing in your area. But when the platform is there, you're not taking advantage of it so people can see you and understand your potential." It was one of the biggest lessons of my career. I was not showing up big when it counted.

My thinking was, *of course everyone sees what I am doing, and they know what I am capable of doing. I'm winning all these awards and accolades at every level, so I am sure people understand my potential.* The truth was that it's all about perception. Even though I was doing the work, everyone didn't know that I was doing it. I had to start sharing my achievements and my skills on a higher level. I don't mean in a boastful or arrogant way, but in a way that helped others and while helping me to stand out among people outside of my direct boss and area team.

> "Change the way you look at things and the things you look at change."
>
> –Wayne W. Dyer

Taking my manager's suggestion, I started speaking up more in meetings. I began to challenge by offering my ideas coupled with anecdotes that made them practical. It made me think differently about my role and the roles that supported our team. I reached back to Aunt Doris and what she'd taught me about strategic thinking and planning. It wasn't enough that I was doing the job and doing it well. I had to do more. I had to think outside of the box of my job description to identify areas where I was able to add value and contribute to the organization as a whole.

Once I started to do that, my exposure and perceptions increased significantly. In the Leadership Discovery Program, I was assigned an executive coach; it was my first experience with one. I expressed my frustrations because I had been an area business leader for five years although it was only slated to be two years. In that role, I had successfully led teams in all five boroughs of New York, Long Island, and the entire State of New Jersey, but I felt stuck. My coach said to me, "Your issue is that they don't look at you as a threat and you accept excuses for why you're not advancing. They have all these excuses and you accept them. The high potential people like you that they believe will leave—they take care of them. How do you ensure that you are visible and that you become a priority? That's your focus."

I took his advice and focused on my visibility even more and made sure I was viewed as a priority. It helped. I was able to secure the role in marketing that I had wanted for so long. Ultimately, this is why I became interested in executive coaching.

Notwithstanding my coveted promotion to the marketing department, it was my investment in other people that really sparked my rise to the next level in the organization. We have an employee resource group (ERG) for people of African ancestry. The VP of human resources and the VP of diversity and inclusion asked if I would chair the group. The problem was that the ERG didn't have the best reputation in the organization. Some people viewed group members as complainers and admonished that I was too upwardly mobile to be associated with the "black group." I was hesitant at first. But I eventually became excited about the opportunity to share all the things I had learned as a high potential that I knew others were not receiving. Moreover, it troubled me more if I were a part of an organization that frowned upon my involvement in an employee resource group focused on African Americans. I decided to step up to the challenge and take on the role of chairman.

My first order of business was to determine the needs of the membership. *What do they need? What are their challenges?* Everyone repeated the same answers. "Well, Marion, we always hear that we're supposed to own our careers, but nobody knows exactly what that means and how to do it." To answer the prevailing need, we created a number of programs that were focused on career development that taught people how to take ownership of their careers and enhance their position within the organization.

I partnered with two human resources specialist to build a full professional development program available for the membership. We implemented the program at evening sessions across the country and the results were immediate. Although the program was created and executed by the African ancestry ERG, all employees were welcome, and we actually had more non-African American attendees than African American. Many participants felt that it was the best development program they had experienced, which caused the executive committee to notice our program. Based on the feedback from the program and its overall impact on employee engagement, the executive committee increased our budget by $600,000 for the execution of more workshops. Shortly thereafter, we implemented a mentoring program for African Americans to gain access to members of the executive committee. It completely transformed the way the organization's upper echelon executives viewed the ERG, and ultimately, me. I rose through the ranks in the marketing division in one of the largest pharmaceutical companies in the world and became the first African American man to become a head of marketing.

After that, I went on to learn so many more valuable lessons, which we will highlight later. My success also reinforced those lessons learned from Sunshine and Aunt Doris. One of the questions I am asked when people find out that I have written this book is, "What motivated you to write it?" It is the notion that investing in other people is the best investment you can ever make. I can honestly say that I have discovered far more than I thought I would in the process.

An experience I had with a client was also a motivating factor in writing this book. She had been with a major media company for over a decade. She was a high performer and felt secure in her role because everyone knew her and her work was good. That all changed when the company reorganized and her new boss was not a fan of her or her work. She said she felt like it was one of those typical situations when someone is promoted to a position, but they don't know as much as some of the employees and so they become intimidated. My client felt that the new boss was setting her up to look incompetent and was trying to build a case for her to be fired.

When we started working together, she was at her wits end and did not know how to handle the situation or what to do next. We worked together for six months and during that time her boss was fired, and she was promoted to a role she had coveted for years.

She came to me and said, "You have to write a book and share what you taught me with more people." I thought she was just being nice until she told me she had started sharing advice she'd learned from me with her coworkers and it was working for them too. She also said, "You know people don't know what they don't know and it's hurting them. Your book will help a lot of people." (Yep, that's where the title came from).

I wasn't sure exactly how to approach the process of writing a book. However, I did know that I didn't want it to be overly academic and sterile. You learn more when you're having fun. I wanted the sense of humor that I have in my coaching sessions to come through in this book. I read an average of fifteen books a year to help me continue to grow and develop as a leader and a coach. I share many of my favorites throughout this book.

I know the question you are asking is, "Is this book for me?" Here is my simple answer; if you are ready to accelerate your career or just increase your impact, or if you have been passed over for a promotion, feel stuck, undervalued, expendable, invisible to leadership, or are consistently frustrated with your boss or coworkers, then this book *is* for you!

You will gain access and insights on how to take ownership of your career; you will have a new awareness of what you control, and how to control it; you will be empowered to maximize your impact and potential; you will receive what the five percent of high potentials receive, plus much more; and finally, you will have access to my support and guidance as you move to the next level in your career.

OVERVIEW

THE FOUR Ps THAT ACCELERATE YOUR CAREER

———◆◆———

Based on my personal experience, training, and now coaching others, I have identified four principles that when applied effectively (you have to do the work), will help accelerate your career. I call them the Four Ps of Success: Performance, Perceptions, Positioning, and Persistence. It is my belief that an aptitude in each of these areas is required to reach the highest level of professional success. All Four Ps are common words, however, in application they are a bit more complex than you might originally think. When you are aware of how to manage each of them effectively, you will own your career and never be a victim of the decisions or indecision of others. In this book, we will define each of these areas and then break them down for everyday application.

Here is a quick overview of the Four Ps:

Performance: We will explore the impact of Emotional Intelligence (EQ) vs. Intelligence Quotient (IQ) on your performance. I will provide an overview of EQ, and you will identify your strengths and areas of opportunity with regard to improving your EQ. You will also identify your triggers and how to manage them in the moment. A high IQ will get you hired, but a high EQ will get you promoted.

Perceptions: Perceptions are how you are viewed by others. We will explore how to establish and maintain an effective personal and professional brand. We will discuss the impact of packaging, body language, and projecting confidence, and how to maximize each of them.

Positioning: In this section we will explore the what, the why—and most importantly—the how of positioning yourself effectively. You can be the best worker, have the highest IQ, and be very perceptive, yet you will not get anywhere if no one knows you. In this section, we review effective networking (where you look like a connector not a parasite), the difference between a sponsor and a mentor, and how to create an effective career plan. We will also explore the impact of the people you have in your network on your positioning within your organization and career.

Persistence: No matter how well you plan, life happens. What separates very talented people who end up with average careers versus those with exceptional careers is persistence. In this section, we will discuss how to discover opportunities in the obstacles in your career (there is always an opportunity in the obstacles; believe me, I know from experience). We also explore how and when it is time to activate your network. If you have put in your work on the first three Ps, you will always have options. Options give us control. And control gives us *power.*

SECTION I—PERFORMANCE

PERFORMANCE
DEFINITION

EMOTIONAL INTELLIGENCE
INCREASES INDIVIDUAL
PERFORMANCE, LEADERSHIP,
AND ORGANIZATIONAL
PRODUCTIVITY.

SOURCE: GEETU BHARWANEY

CHAPTER 1

The Impact of EQ vs. IQ

We all know those super smart kids from school that you run into ten years later, and somehow their supernatural intelligence didn't necessarily manifest into success in business, or sometimes, life in general. It's because although one's Intelligence Quotient (IQ) is a solid indicator of an ability to perform well in school and an institutional learning environment, it is not often a great predictor of future success in business.

Here's what we know about IQ:

1. It predicts school grades very well

2. It does not predict success in life well

3. It is a poor predictor of job success

4. It peaks in our late teens

Historically, a great deal of importance was placed on someone's IQ, but modern research has shown that a person's IQ only contributes to twenty to thirty percent (20-30%) of a leader's success.[1] To

---

1 Reldan S. Nadler, PsyD, *Leading with Emotional Intelligence* (New York: McGraw Hill, 2011).

look solely at someone's capacity in that regard negates qualities that have proven to be far more important and better indicators of success.

> "People with a growth mind-set believe that they can improve with effort. They outperform those with a fixed mind-set, even when they have a lower IQ, because they embrace challenges, treating them as opportunities to learn something new."
>
> —Travis Bradbery

On the other hand, Emotional Intelligence or Emotional Quotient (EQ) is widely viewed as the strongest predictor of success in the work world. Most people have heard the term Emotional Intelligence or have been told it is important, but the vast majority of people are not aware of what good EQ looks like and how to assess and manage themselves to improve their EQ. I have found that even some high potentials have received feedback on needing to improve aspects of their EQ, but not the requisite tools or insights to improve. If you miss the EQ part of Performance, you will never succeed in executing the other three Ps because EQ is the foundation to overall success.

Peter Salovey and John Mayer introduced the term "Emotional Intelligence" in 1990 with it gaining popularity with Daniel Goleman's

1995 book, *Emotional Intelligence.*[2] Goleman defines EQ as follows: "The capacity for recognizing our own feelings and those of others, for motivating ourselves, and for managing emotions well in ourselves and in our relationships." Most intelligent people think; "I'm smart enough, therefore, I will be successful," and they are correct to a degree. However, they never reach their full potential until they begin to understand themselves and their impact on other people, and until they are able to identify the different variables within their environment to manage them effectively. As I said previously, my mother is one of the smartest people I know; however, her emotional intelligence was something that she had to develop. I also had to develop my EQ just ask some of my fraternity brothers from my undergraduate years. Truly successful people are both intellectually and emotionally intelligent. They have high IQs and even higher EQs. There are a lot of smart people out there, so being smart and doing "your job" is the price of entry into the conversation. The price of entry is not viewed as something that makes you special or differentiates you from the crowd—it is expected.

As the study of and focus on EQ began to take flight, many researchers started evaluating and breaking down the formula for success in terms of IQ and EQ. Here is the current success equation breakdown based on years of research:

---

2 Nadler, 7.

EQ + IQ

80% + 20%

SUCCESS

When you look at the equation, there's a greater percentage of success that is focused on EQ than is on IQ. Some experts like Salovey and Mayer say that the breakdown is 80/20 while others like Nadler say it's 70/30, but they all agree that the predominant factor in success is EQ. While you were in school and still learning, IQ was the important determining factor toward your potential success. You also learned about work ethic, focus, and dedication that enhanced your IQ. For the most part, you didn't have to engage your emotional intelligence to earn good grades unless you were involved in a group project, and even in that situation you were only responsible for your part of the project. Once you enter the business world, or adult relationships in general, there is a significant component of your success and outcomes that will be based on your emotional intelligence.

IQ GETS YOU HIRED

EQ GETS YOU PROMOTED

A research study was conducted with business leaders to understand why qualified people aren't promoted. Here are the top three reasons:

- Lack of social skills
- Inability to take criticism
- Lack of motivation to keep learning

The first two are clearly EQ related and the third has to do with managing perceptions, which is covered later.

People with higher EQs enjoy the following benefits:

- Career advancement
- Increased confidence
- Greater job satisfaction
- Being viewed as a team builder and a problem solver
- Higher performance

The good news is that EQ can be learned while IQ is a static indicator of a specific ability that will only fluctuate up or down slightly with education and experience. The first step to improving your EQ is to understand the four core components or quadrants. The four quadrants of the Emotional Competencies Model (below) are fundamental in assessing your present EQ and determining areas for growth.

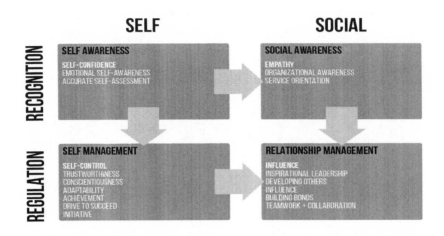

In order to gain a cursory understanding, you need to be aware that this model is concerned with two factors on the horizontal line—self and others. And two factors on the vertical line—awareness and actions. Emotionally intelligent people manage themselves and their environment more effectively to get the outcomes they desire.

One of the simplest definitions of emotional intelligence is: The ability to recognize and control your emotions while recognizing the emotions of others in an effort to use the information to manage interactions. With regard to the four key competencies, another helpful definition is "exhibiting a good balance of personal and social competencies in four distinct areas or clusters:

Self-Awareness—Understanding Yourself
Self-Management—Managing Yourself
Social Awareness—Understanding Others

Relationship Management—Managing [Interactions with] Others"[3]

The key word in the definition is balance. It's rare that anyone is a high achiever in all four areas all the time. But a good balance of the four is necessary to communicate and perform effectively within an organization. Emotional intelligence is predicated upon leveraging your self-awareness and the awareness of your environment in order to stay focused and to accomplish your objectives and goals. The foundational characteristic of emotional intelligence is self-awareness. It is the bedrock of emotional intelligence. If you don't have self-awareness, then the other three key competencies will be difficult.

Self-Awareness

Learn to understand yourself and the triggers that drive you from productive to unproductive. It takes making a determination of what your core values are and developing the ability to take a step back to ask yourself specific questions to remain on track toward your objective. If you lack self-awareness, your emotions tend to control the situation and you may react in situations where it's neither productive nor personal. If you feel that the events and circumstances of your life are consistently the fault of others, or if you are constantly the victimized person in a situation, then you probably need to take a closer look at your level of self-awareness. The truth is that everything in your life starts and ends with *you*.

Self-Management

Once you become self-aware, you're in a much better position to practice thoughtful self-management. Understand all of those aspects of self, and then be able to do something about them. It is one thing to understand, and it's another thing to be able to exhibit control.

---

3 Nadler, 7.

Social Awareness

Social awareness means having the ability to understand and respond to the needs of others. Improve your social skills and gain the respect of others as you apply these concepts. Understanding other people›s feelings is central to emotional intelligence. Get it wrong and you'll be seen as uncaring and insensitive.

Relationship Management

Relationship management is using awareness of your emotions and those of others to manage interactions successfully. Relationship management involves clear communication and effective handling of conflict. It is about building and maintaining healthy relationships to help you become more productive and impactful.

Practical Applications and Anecdotes

Throughout this book, I share stories from experiences over the years. Of course, the names and details are creatively altered, but the lessons are the same. We all love a great story because they illustrate learning points vividly and can be entertaining. More importantly, I believe that an anecdotal reference has a far greater impact than pages of information and research.

Now that you understand the basics of emotional intelligence, it is time for a story…and there's no better place to start than with the man in the mirror. One of the crystallizing moments for me related to emotional intelligence was when I moved from being a sales manager into marketing. I went into an important meeting with my new boss and an entirely new group of coworkers. It was significant because it was one of the banner cross-functional events at the company. Internally, I was very critical of the presenter. I remember thinking the entire time, *OMG, what is this man talking about? He's all over the place and is not making sense.* It was how I felt, but I knew better than to express it outwardly. Or, at least I thought I wasn't expressing it out-wardly. Turns out I was very transparent in what I felt.

> If you're going to be a leader, then you're going to have to be able to understand what you're projecting, not just what you're saying.

Following the meeting, my new manager asked me back to her office. She said, "I want to give you some feedback. You didn't like that presentation." She was right, but I didn't know it was that obvious. It was true that I didn't understand how anyone could have found value in that presentation. "You thought he was disorganized, somewhat incompetent, and that someone needed to take charge in that meeting because it was just going off of the rails."

You could've picked my jaw off of the floor because that was exactly what I had been thinking, but I was confused. *How did she know?*

When I asked, she said, "It was all over your face and in your body language. You said exactly that without ever needing to speak one single word and everyone in the room including the speaker knew it. If you're going to reach your potential as a leader you are going to have to be able to understand what you're projecting and not just what you're saying. You looked just as bad as the speaker did today."

It was the first time that it resonated with me that it's more than just what you say or do. My lack of self-awareness and social awareness impaired my ability to manage my reactions and emotions in that meeting.

My manager was grooming me for higher-level leadership positions in the company by illustrating the importance of emotional intelligence on my prospects for advancement. Too many people have the mistaken belief that if they do a great job and perform well, then they will be promoted and/or pinpointed for acceleration within an organization. The truth is that just because you're good at your job doesn't mean that you are going to succeed to the level of your full potential or that you are ready to motivate and lead others. It just doesn't work that way. I see a lot of people being promoted because of their technical skills, but they go on to fail miserably at the next level because of their lack of EQ.

I'm sure some of you can think of managers or executives who lack emotional intelligence and still manage to climb the ranks. Anyone who has ever had a job has at least one horror story of a manager or executive who exhibited a total lack of control.

Let's talk about a woman we will call Kathy. She was a vice president at an entertainment company who was pegged from the beginning as a high potential achiever because of her educational pedigree—double Ivy League undergraduate and graduate degrees with honors. Kathy was not someone who screamed and yelled at employees. She was, however, very intimidating, and used intimidation as her means of getting people to perform. She had many grievances against her, which ultimately led to the company terminating her. Due to her pervasive reputation in the entertainment industry, she was unable to secure a similar position for nearly two years. During that time, she made the great decision to take a sabbatical to get executive and emotional intelligence coaching, leadership training, and do other development work. She totally changed her style and is now in a senior leadership role with another organization. Emotional intelligence was far more important than her degrees, her achievements, and certainly her IQ.

These days Kathy's reputation within her industry different. She is known for being a solution-oriented p Her employees compliment her leadership style as being tive" and "much more open." Kathy's termination and shu the industry led her to take a hard and fast look at her e...otional intelligence. Although she was by all assessments intellectually brilliant, she would never have arrived back in the industry—let alone the C-Suite—had she not worked on her émotional intelligence. She got there by increasing her emotional intelligence in a manner consistent with the equation presented at the beginning of this chapter.

Now that you have a foundational understanding of emotional intelligence and some real-life examples of how important emotional intelligence is to your career, it is time for you to start evaluating where you stand currently.

SUMMARY

1. EQ is a far better indicator of your success than IQ. Being smart will get you a job, but EQ will get you promoted.

2. The two of three primary reasons qualified people are not promoted involve the lack of EQ: 1) The lack of social skills, and 2) The inability to take criticism. (The third reason unrelated to EQ is the lack of motivation to keep learning.)

3. You can increase your EQ through awareness and practice (doing the work).

4. There are four key components of EQ: Self-Awareness, Self-Management, Social Awareness, and Relationship Management.

5. Self-Awareness is the bedrock of EQ.

a. Relationships matter in any business. You can't foster healthy and beneficial relationships without a high EQ.

EXERCISE

Here are some steps you can take:

1. Keep a journal for one week of your interactions at work or home that didn't go as well as you would have liked.

2. Each day, reflect on the situation(s) and visualize the outcome being exactly what you would have preferred.

3. Now, write down one or two things you could have done differently to get that ideal outcome.

CHAPTER 2

Did You Build Your Own Ceiling?

Now that you have the basics of EQ down and have started to think about where you are in relation to the four quadrants, it is time to dig deeper so you know how to identify what is happening and to make emotionally intelligent choices.

I was maybe five or six years old when I started to understand the difference between the manner in which my grandmother engaged the world and the way in which my mother did. My mother would yell, curse, and scream at everyone, but mostly at my grandmother. Looking back, my mother certainly lacked emotional intelligence. My grandmother, on the other hand, demonstrated so much control when interacting with my mother, and she continued to invest in us as if she were unaffected by my mother's abuse. This is my first recollection of the differentiation between effective and desired behavior models versus ineffective and undesired ones. I knew then that I wanted to be more like my grandmother, than like my mother. I had no idea what Sunshine did to stay calm and focused in those moments, but I knew it made her look like the person in charge, the person in control, and I wanted to be that person. So, I started to watch and study everything she did. But as I grew older, I realized that my reactions were a lot more like my mother than my grandmother. I had work to do, and I had no idea what I didn't know was hurting me!

I've found that far too many people become victims of their situation, of other people, or of what someone else did. Moving toward increased emotional intelligence turns the lens back to evaluating how you are processing and then responding versus reacting to the situation. The more aware you become and the calmer you are when responding to a situation, the more impactful and effective you will be. For example, when someone aggressively and negatively reacts to another person's actions, that person has surrendered control. They've allowed the amygdala to react.

I know you may be thinking, "Wait one minute, that's an SAT word." The amygdala is the part of your brain that manages the fight-or-flight conditioning. It is our primitive reaction mechanism. Without getting too scientific, the amygdalae (singular: amygdala) are two almond-shaped groups of nuclei located deep and medially within the temporal lobes of the brain.[4] Research indicates that the amygdalae are associated with fear conditioning that is associated with negative memory. Studies have shown that the amygdala has a strong connection with emotional learning.

In layman's terms, when your amygdala is dictating your actions, you're reacting based on fear triggering your most primitive reaction—fight-or-flight. This worked for the cavemen and cavewomen, but we are not facing saber tooth tigers at work (well most of us aren't). Still the amygdala evaluates every threat as life or death and reacts accordingly. I don't want to sound like the amygdala is not needed today; it is definitely needed in a crisis where you have to make a split-second decision. But at work, in a meeting or a conversation with a peer, it is not life or death.

---

4 *Merriam-Webster's Collegiate Dictionary,* 11th ed. (Springfield, MA: Merriam-Webster, Inc., 2004).

When the amygdala is in charge, we call it an amygdala hijack. When that occurs, you have given up control to the other person or the situation, and they are now dictating your behavior. They are in control of you and your behavior; and as Janet Jackson said, "I want to be the one in control!"

How does the amygdala impact IQ? I'm glad you asked. When you are in an amygdala hijack, you not only lose control, but you also lose IQ points. Research[5] shows that during an amygdala hijack we lose ten to twenty IQ points. This means that your argument is weaker, and you are less articulate in delivering your message. It is never a good thing to lose IQ points.

People with high EQs are able to manage the amygdala and maintain control by activating their prefrontal cortex in the heat of the moment. The prefrontal cortex is the portion of the brain where complex thinking and problem solving occur. The prefrontal cortex's basic activity is considered to be the orchestration of thoughts and actions in accordance with internal goals.[6] It is the part of your brain activity where you actually think things through and make executive decisions based on your objectives or real data, not pure emotion. If you solely rely on that primitive component of your brain in tough or uncomfortable situations, you will derail your career, and, more importantly, you can sever important relationships and drive negative perceptions. I will help you understand how to activate your prefrontal cortex, which is a skill that will separate you from the crowd. It will also keep you in control like Janet.

Emotionally intelligent people stay composed during stressful situations and are able to evaluate as well as choose the best option (prefrontal) versus reacting out of primitive emotions (amygdala hijacking). This means that emotional intelligence starts and ends with you.

Once you have self-awareness, and then self-control, you can start managing your environment more effectively. It's one thing to be aware, but it's another thing to execute. Everyone is on the spectrum of

---

5 Reldan S. Nadler, PsyD, "Where Did My IQ Points Go?" *Psychology Today* (April 29, 2011).
6 David H. Freedman and Earl K. Miller, "A Comparison of Primate Prefrontal and Inferior Tempural Cortices during Visual Categorization," *The Journal of Neuroscience* (June 15, 2003).

proficiency in at least one of the four competencies to some degree. No one is one hundred percent proficient in all four competencies or completely deficient in all four. For some people, empathy and awareness are innate, while most of us need to develop these skills through self-assessment, coaching, and practice. High potential achievers are often provided the resources and tools to develop the skills necessary for success, while others are left behind. Quite frankly, it's not hard to develop the skills once you examine your starting point. We'll go through each of the four competencies so that you can identify areas of strength and areas of opportunity for growth. I'll also provide an assessment to see how close you are to being proficient in each area. Once you are able to do that, you can use the tools presented here to grow in the same ways as high potential achievers.

Self-Awareness

As indicated, self-awareness is the bedrock of emotional intelligence. Your ability to accurately and honestly assess your emotional reactions to situations is paramount to growing your emotional intelligence. One of the questions I am often asked is, "What does low self-awareness look like in day-to-day interactions?" A person with low self-awareness rarely takes ownership of their responsibility in a situation. A key sign that someone lacks self-awareness is when they constantly make excuses for their bad behavior. They make statements like, "this is just who or how I am" or "it was her fault (that happened)." Focus on your understanding of the part you play in the situation and fix yourself first. People are quick to blame someone else but are slow to claim their part.

Nadler says, "[Self-awareness] is the awareness of your strengths and weaknesses, your mood, your varying feelings, your behavior, your impact on others, your pattern, and your personal story. Once aware you are better able to manage, monitor, regulate, and control your reactions to situations."[7]

---

7 Nadler, *Leading with Emotional Intelligence,* p. 33.

One thing I do want to make clear is the difference between being self-aware and being self-critical. Self-critical is just beating yourself up. Be careful not to do that when evaluating yourself. Being self-critical is another way of becoming a victim (*I never do anything right, no one likes me,* and so on). A great book I often recommend to clients who desire (or need) growth in self-awareness is *Change Your Questions, Change Your Life*[8], by Marilee Adams. Adams stresses the importance of managing the stories you tell yourself about yourself and about other people. For example, if you interview for a position that you know you are qualified for, but don't get the role, then possible negative questions you ask yourself are:

- Why do they keep overlooking me?
- Why are they so unfair?
- How could this happen to me again?

However, the questions asked by a self-aware person are focused on moving forward and growing; and they are very different. A self-aware person asks:

- What went well in that situation?
- What could I have done differently?
- Where are the opportunities for me to grow and get even better at X?
- What will I do differently in the future?
- Was it them or me?
- What are my options now and going forward?

Being self-aware is about taking ownership and building on positive indicators versus focusing on negative indicators. People don't expect perfection, but they do look for some self-awareness so that when a mistake is made, you demonstrate a capacity for improvement. The person who doesn't make the same mistake twice is

---

8 Marilee Adams, PhD, *Change Your Questions Change Your Life*, Second Edition (San Francisco: Berrett-Koehler Publishers, Inc., 2009).

revered while the person who repeatedly makes the same mistakes is viewed as incompetent.

When you focus on building your positive attributes, it gives you an opportunity to maintain those and make adjustments around your "derailers" because most people don't need to start from scratch. A "derailer" is defined as a behavior or attitude that curtails an individual's performance or advancement.[9] We all have positive indicators that have allowed us to develop. It's about reaching the next level, and that generally doesn't require a complete behavioral and personality overhaul. For example, let's say you have ten positive indicators of proficiency and you have two areas of opportunity. If you put all your focus and energy on those two, then you're losing impact in some of the ten positive indicators. Instead, by focusing on your positives—so that they balance out those two areas of opportunity—you have the chance to have twelve positive indicators. There has to be an evaluation of how you can leverage those positives to address some of your areas of opportunity.

A great example of my own self-awareness evolution was at the beginning of my leadership development program. The feedback I received in my 360° evaluations was very positive from my peers and direct reports, but my manager rated me low on executive presence. I was surprised; and honestly, a bit ticked off. I thought, *I'm doing everything right to lead my team and help my peers. I had good stage presence and exhibited confidence. How could he say that I lacked executive presence?!* My executive coach who was reviewing the information with me recommended that I speak with my manager to gain insight (not to defend what I had done). When I spoke to my manager, he said I was playing small when it counted the most with senior leadership. He further explained that I was taking a passive listener position in those meetings, where, in fact, there were opportunities for greater visibility throughout the organization. I wasn't sharing any of the ideas that I had privately shared with my manager and colleagues. I wasn't asking provocative or impactful questions that

---

9 *Merriam-Webster's.*

illustrated my interest and focus on the success of the organization. My manager said, "By failing to do all of those things, you were not demonstrating an executive presence on a national level that you had exhibited on the regional level."

I had no idea that I was not showing up with the right presence; and in fact, I should be saying more because a lot of my ideas were intuitive to me. I figured everyone knew what I knew, and it wouldn't add anything valuable to the meetings. I was unaware that my behavior was viewed as passive and not indicative of the executive that I intended to be. I took a moment to evaluate what I was doing correctly in my regional and smaller group meetings, and then I identified opportunities where I could apply those strengths to the larger meetings where I needed to show more leadership qualities and executive presence.

I started preparing more effectively for those opportunities. For example, I started reviewing the agendas early on and identified key initiatives or processes that I or my team were developing, which I could use as an example to reinforce a concept or offer as an alternative perspective. I planned some questions based on the agenda that I genuinely wanted answered, and I thought would add value to the meeting. I also adjusted my placement during meetings so that I was more visible by sitting in the front. And it worked. Managers from different parts of the country started calling me. They wanted to know more about what I was doing and how my team was executing these initiatives. The results showed that taking the time to self-assess created new leadership opportunities for me.

It would have been easy for me to become a victim. But you cannot be a victim while also being self-aware. My response to my manager's feedback affected the opportunities that I received from it. If I had reacted as a victim (blaming someone else for my predicament), the outcome would have been completely different. Had I taken the position that he was picking on me or being unfair, I would not have had the wherewithal to self-assess and to see that he was absolutely correct. Self-awareness is the bedrock of emotional intelligence because if you don't realize what you're doing and why you're doing it, you'll never be able to change it. And there is no way you'll ever have a great social lens if you don't have an astute internal lens. Similarly, there is no way you can really manage relationships effectively if you're not aware of your impact and how to control it. As long as you are a victim of someone else's behavior and don't take ownership of what you're doing or could do, you won't find different options or alternatives to be more effective. This is true whether it's in controlling yourself or managing relationships.

Self-Management

Self-management—*noun*—management of or by oneself, the taking of responsibility for one's own behavior and well-being.[10]

Effective self-management skills have the power to dramatically change almost every aspect of our lives. For this reason, self-management skills are some of the most important *and* difficult skills to learn in business, in the workplace, and in our personal lives. Self-management refers to our ability to control feelings, emotions, and ultimately actions. It plays a decisive role in business and our trajectory for success. Self-awareness is the bedrock of emotional intelligence, whereas self-management is the catalyst that elevates the awareness to effectiveness. It's one thing to know something about yourself (self-awareness); however, it is much more important to do something different with what you know and change your behavior (self-management). I have coached clients who have improved upon or already had good self-awareness, but they are reluctant to do something different to garner different results. That is the key of self-management—taking a different action step that results in a more desirable outcome.

---

10 *Merriam-Webster's.*

> "Self-management is the catalyst that elevates the awareness to effectiveness."

The key to understanding self-management is to identify your triggers that turn into those derailers. Once you identify what your triggers are, then you can actively pinpoint when you're starting to feel them and then manage your response. When you feel an emotion coming on or when someone has hit one of your trigger points, you are more readily able to stop and correct the course. This reflects back to using the prefrontal cortex versus the amygdala and not reacting to the trigger, but instead thinking through your response with your objective in mind. If after a situation you say to yourself, "I can't believe I did that," you know that you triggered your amygdala. You failed to manage yourself and respond effectively to that situation.

Self-management simply is bringing down the emotions and bringing up the thinking. For example, when you're feeling a trigger, take a deep breath, pause, and listen to the other person to understand their point. Identify that a trigger has been initiated and take a moment to think versus reacting.

Here is where a book, *The Four Agreements,* proved to be very helpful in the personal development of my self-management skills. In this best-selling book, author Don Miguel Ruiz reveals the source of self-limiting beliefs that steal joy and perpetuate suffering. Selling over six million copies and counting, *The Four Agreements* relies on ancient teachings and wisdom to inform a modern exploration of personal freedom and success. It teaches us ways to disconnect from the beliefs and agreements we have made with ourselves and others that limit our happiness, success, and joy.

The Four Agreements are as follows:

1. Be impeccable with your word.
2. Don't take anything personally.
3. Don't make assumptions.
4. Always do your best.[11]

If you haven't, I highly recommend that you read the entire book, for it will truly impact the way you interact with yourself and the world in the simplest, seemingly common-sense ways. If you're like me, then you will have page after page of awakened moments that, though they are stated so plainly, never occurred to you before reading them. In the context of self-awareness and self-management, two of the four agreements stand out as being key:

- **"Don't Take Anything Personally**. Nothing others do is because of you. What others say and do is a projection of their own reality, their own dreams. When you are immune to the opinions and actions of others, you won't be the victim of needless suffering.
- **Don't Make Assumptions**. Find the courage to ask questions and to express what you really want. Communicate with others as clearly as you can to avoid misunderstandings, sadness, and drama. With just this one agreement, you can completely transform your life.[12]"

If you take a moment to evaluate why you are reacting negatively to a situation, you will more than likely discover that you're taking it personally and/or you're making assumptions about the situation or the other person's intentions and motives. *Stop! Don't!*

---

11 Don Miguel Ruiz, *The Four Agreements* (San Francisco: Amber-Allen Publishing, Inc., 1997).
12 Ruiz.

I use this exercise to activate my prefrontal cortex in order to better manage my actions once triggered:

1. Why am I feeling X? (attacked, disrespected, overlooked, ignored, discounted…)

2. Okay, I'm feeling X, but why? (I am afraid I might look bad, they will think they are getting over on me, I don't like bullies…)

3. What can I do now to stay in the moment and in control? (How do I communicate directly and show empathy for their point of view? What are they saying that I can agree with and build on to put us back on topic?)

This process gives you the space to realize that you're upset because you're taking what's being said or done too personally, but it's not personal. The other person is trying to assert or defend something based on his or her own background and experience. Once you stop taking other people's words or actions personally, you can then manage yourself and your emotions. *Am I trying to win or am I looking for a win-win? Am I trying to be right or am I trying to be happy?* If you are looking for a win-win or you're trying to be happy, the best thing for you to do is not to react negatively. Again, the foundation of self-management is bringing down the emotion and bringing up thinking by understanding when you have been triggered and looking for other options to accomplish your objective. That is your primary focus in self-management.

Many researchers and coaches use the terms self-management and self-control interchangeably. I do agree that self-control is a component of self-management, but self-management is a higher goal. You can control yourself by not saying or doing anything, which is not always the best option. Management takes the idea a step further because you are then looking for alternative ways to approach and act on any given situation or issue. Practicing self-management keeps you focused on working toward your objective. Self-control is not reacting negatively, which is the first step.

Here is my personal definition of self-management:

Self-management is applying self-control to actively identify the best options for you to reach your objective or goal.

There is no denying that self-management takes work. You have to be honest with yourself, which is definitely easier said than done. You shouldn't walk the journey alone though. Use the people around you to help you identify your strength areas and opportunities for growth. Undoubtedly, those surrounding you, both at work and at home, have an opinion. Self-awareness and self-management require a bit of vulnerability, which is also a growth opportunity. The same way you pose questions to yourself, ask the same of others. Explain that you're working on your self-awareness and self-management and you'd like their thoughts on how you show up for meetings, at home, in conflict, and so on. You should seek as much feedback as possible from a variety of people you trust. Lastly, look for the consistency or common denominators in their feedback.

I like to start with a very basic question that is not loaded with your expectations about the response. "When I come into a room, what do I bring with me?" This question opens up the door for a variety of answers depending on whom you are asking. Once you receive answers, stay open, and follow-up with more specific questions that help you further elicit how the person perceives what you bring into the room with you.

Again, openness and honesty are key for the process to work. I would even challenge you to approach someone you have not worked well with and let them know you're working on being a better partner. It is also a great way to engage your boss or advisor, as you will ultimately turn them into a collaborator and champion. In addition to your strengths and areas of opportunity, be sure to identify characteristics that could be derailers. Once you have compiled enough feedback and drawn out the consistencies, find partners with whom you can work to help reach your full potential. Seek partners who will tell you when you're making improvements and when you've reverted to derailing behavior. Now, you can't digest every bit of feedback because some of it will likely be poisonous or ill intended. But you will be able to effectively decipher what is rich and what is ill based on the consistency of the feedback.

Social Awareness

Once you've mastered—or begun to master—the objectives of self-awareness and self-management, it is time to consider your relationships with other people. The difference between self-awareness and social awareness is moving from understanding yourself to understanding the impact you have on other people and the impact they have on you. The objective is empathy as well as understanding how you can ultimately manage your relationships to achieve your common objective (relationship management). Social awareness also includes developing an understanding of the politics and dynamics within your organization and beginning to leverage that knowledge to achieve your goals.

Some people are extremely socially aware and learned empathy early on in life. If that's not natural for you, practicing it just like you practice self-awareness will sharpen your skill. This time, however, the focus is on other people and not solely on yourself. It requires a great deal of listening and observation (80% listening and 20% speaking). Empathy means paying attention to people's body language, their tone of voice, and the words they use. It means being in tune with outward reactions to a situation, and it is the beginning of developing social awareness skills. Yet, social awareness is not about judgment; it is about putting yourself in the other person's shoes to understand their motivations as well as their objectives. Being socially aware means you have a heightened perceptiveness about your surroundings.

One of my coaching clients was in a contentious situation when he took over as the head of a department in his organization. One of the teams in the company was relaying information to the internal groups that he didn't feel accurately depicted the entire picture. From his perspective, the product was not doing well when he took over, and it was a misrepresentation of where the company was with it. In fact, the company had received a great deal of negative consumer feedback based on the inaccurate information the team was providing. It was a major misstep from a marketing standpoint, and it was my client's job to correct the course to not only accurately reflect the data but also to regain consumer confidence in the product and in the company's statements about the product.

I told my client that he should take a step back and do some research so that he was fully informed about the landscape before proceeding. He discovered there was a huge disconnect between what the sales team was utilizing as the basis for their presentations and what was accurate. Many members of the sales team had also complained about the inaccuracy of the information. Seemingly, my client's team and the team that provided the information had two conflicting goals. The other team's goal was to present a successful percentage of access to the executive committee, and his focus was on the customer. By the time they arrived at the meeting to discuss it all from both sides, it was highly contentious. At first, they went back and forth about what was accurate and what was not. He said the discussions became really heated until he realized that he'd been triggered and that he was not going to win the argument because the tension was too high. Utilizing the techniques we had gone over, he took a breath, paused, and then realized they were merely trying to defend their jobs. He turned the lens from what he was aiming to accomplish and understand to what they were trying to accomplish. He had to find a middle ground that suited both teams and that allowed the entire team to reach its objective, which was to market this product to consumers successfully and to provide excellent service to customers.

In our coaching session, I encouraged my client to come up with a way to benefit all of the objectives. He devised a plan to redefine what access meant when communicating with the executive committee versus coverage when communicating to customers. This allowed both sides to achieve their goals. Magically, they aligned because he went from focusing only on his goal to having empathy for their position. He had basically been saying *your baby is ugly and you're a liar*. Of course, they weren't going to react favorably to that— no one would.

By finding a win-win, both teams were happy and eventually the executive committee decided the company needed to change the way they defined the product information. Based on that, he created an entirely new program that other teams within the organization began to follow. It became a company-wide initiative that course corrected so many internal disagreements.

Utilizing his social awareness skills, my client created an opportunity for growth, not only for those two teams, but also throughout the entire organization. The through line in all of this is to focus on your objective and how your behavior, reactions and perceptions either move you closer to your objective or push you further away. First, you have to be clear on your objective and work your way from there. If your objective is to win, be right, or flex your muscles, you are setting yourself up for an unnecessary battle. You may win the battle, but the true question is: *are you winning the war of career success*?

One (true) corporate urban legend, if you will, that perfectly illustrates how an executive's emotional unintelligence will eventually catch up with them is one of my favorite stories. It is the story of Jack, the mid-level manager who'd been with an insurance company for many years. Jack had an industry-wide reputation of being a bully. He yelled and screamed at everyone. His leadership style was intimidation, and he achieved what he wanted from his direct reports and colleagues by wearing them down until they submitted. Everyone was scared of him, but he was highly intelligent and delivered to the bottom line.

Every year, Jack surpassed his goals, and without fail, he won service awards based purely on the numbers. It was a bit of a disincentive to other employees because he was consistently rewarded despite his appalling behavior. Jack couldn't keep employees on his team, and when the economy took a downturn, the insurance company he worked for had to do layoffs. Guess who was one of the first managers to be laid off? Yep, you got it right—Jack.

Needless to say, Jack was furious and didn't understand why he was being laid off considering he had outperformed his peers year after year. The company decided that it was more important to keep managers who encouraged respect and a sense of community as the company downsized. The company wanted to retain managers who could produce the same results by motivating their team versus driving them to exhaustion like Jack was known to do.

It wasn't purely an altruistic concern that motivated top executives though. Jack's behavior also had some significant bottom line effects—turnover. It is very expensive to replace employees: severance, loss of manpower hours, and hiring and training new employees, just to name a few factors. Managers who better exhibited emotional intelligence than Jack saved those key bottom line costs.

Like so many in Jack's position, he figured that he'd gotten that far doing it that way, so he saw no need to make adjustments… until it was too late. The point that Jack missed was that this was as far as he was going to get with that type of behavior—nothing higher than a mid-level position was on the horizon for him. As the legend goes, Jack had to change careers and industries entirely because the damage he had done to his reputation was irreparable within his company and ultimately, his whole industry.

Relationship Management

The key to successful relationship management is to look for win-wins in every situation instead of trying to secure a win just for yourself and your team. For this reason, it is the bowtie that connects all three of the previous competencies. It is the end part because it is the consideration of how you leverage the first three competencies to make sure you're not only meeting your objectives, but you're also building solid relationships and influencing others. Relationships are essential and the most important thing to achieving success in both your professional and personal life. You achieve your objectives through effective management, maintenance, and how you leverage your relationships. However, relationship management does not stand alone because one of the components of relationship management is social awareness, which as I said means stepping outside of yourself to consider other people's perspectives and position. Start by asking yourself questions that build empathy. *What are they thinking? What are their motivations? What are they trying to achieve?*

> "You can make more friends in two months by becoming interested in other people than you can in two years by trying to get other people interested in you."
>
> –Dale Carnegie

Once you understand that relationship management is about looking at your own objective and determining an approach that satisfies both sets of goals, then you can effectively manage the relationship. Or, at the very least, you can acknowledge their needs/perspective, which also leads to effective relationship management. Relationship management includes changing your style of communication, compromising areas that are less important to your objective, and more times than not, empowering the other person by acknowledging the value and validity of their point of view. Like my client in the previous example did. When I say this in coaching sessions or at work, people believe that I am asking them to be insincere or phony. That couldn't be further from the truth. What I am saying is that you employ a different mind-set. Think *and* versus *or*.

Here is an example: "How do I stay firm on the outcome we need to accomplish *and* also demonstrate understanding or compassion for the other person's point of view?" Asking this simple "and question" to yourself will activate your prefrontal cortex and expand the number of options. With that said, you have to be true to your objective, too. If you don't maintain your integrity in these situations, no one will trust you. If people don't trust you, then you don't have positive relationships with them. Instead, you want to look for commonalities to help reach the desired outcome. You don't want to lie or cower down. What you want to do is find an effective way to communicate, engage, *and* make sure the other person feels empowered, all the while maintaining your power, voice, and respect. It boils down to looking for different options and not just doing things one way, or your way. Being phony is telling someone what he or she wants to hear, despite disagreeing with what you're saying. That's not effective relationship management because you're not going to feel good about it. At the end of effective relationship management, both people feel good and respected. You may still disagree; however, you've found a way to disagree that creates a win-win situation, or at least choose the best possible outcome.

A key component to relationship management is being able to listen with genuine interest and understanding, instead of listening for an opportunity to reinforce your point on why the other person is wrong. The latter will entrench you deeper in your own perspective and why you're right. If you listen from the lens of genuinely wanting to understand what the other person is saying, eventually you will find common ground, and you will be able to identify win-win scenarios that make everyone happy.

Mostly, people want to be heard and to know that they matter. They want to feel their opinions are respected and therefore, you must respect them. Once you build an environment of mutual respect and trust, anything is possible. You will never get the best answers without the best questions. Your questions need to have quality and the right intention behind them. The only way to achieve that is to actively and genuinely listen to the other person's point of view as well as their goals.

A common misconception about emotional intelligence is that it only pertains to people like Jack, who had the ability to lose his cool. On the contrary, a need for a heightened sense of emotional intelligence can also manifest itself in people who never raise their voice and—for all intents and purposes—are in control socially. A case in point is another highly intelligent coaching client. In one of our first sessions, I let her unload about the difficult time she was having with her boss. By her account, her boss was incompetent and consistently sent her email messages filled with inaccurate assessments and feedback. My client's response was to reply to these emails correcting the inaccuracies and pointing out where she believed her boss had unfairly targeted her and her performance. She also let her boss know that she had been documenting all their interactions that she found to be outside of protocol or unfair. Basically, she was telling her boss that she didn't know what she was doing and that she was untrustworthy. Needless to say, that did not go over well.

A key marker of an emotionally intelligent person is the ability to identify alternative ways to achieve their objective with a win-win outcome in mind.

I discussed her level of emotional intelligence, but she was not accepting of it. She believed that since she was not yelling, screaming, or acting out that she was not emotionally unintelligent. Yet, sending inappropriate counterpunch emails to her boss was just as emotionally unintelligent as yelling at her co-workers. She didn't understand that emotional intelligence is about communication and understanding her position on the team. She felt she was in a fight and had to defend herself, but the contentious relationship she was creating with her boss was toxic and affecting others' perceptions of her performance. She needed to find alternative ways to get her point across effectively. Up to that point, she had not successfully done so. Her behavior demonstrated a lack of emotional intelligence. A key marker of an emotionally intelligent person is the ability to identify alternative ways to achieve their objectives with a win-win outcome in mind.

Pulling It All Together

George is a perfect example of someone who did an exceptional job but was failing in the area of emotional intelligence. When we first began working together, he brought in double the revenue of not only everyone else on his team, but nationwide throughout his organization. At the nuts and bolts of the job, he was fantastic. Still, he had been sitting by as people with lesser skills and results were getting promoted instead of him. He assumed that the issue was a jealous boss who was intimidated by him. His boss even told him point blank that when management level positions opened up, he had no intention of recommending him for a promotion despite his stellar performance.

Once we began coaching, I quickly realized that George lacked social awareness and self-management. In fact, his self-management was very low. While being an advocate for his customers, he frequently lost his cool with the representatives of third-party agencies. Although this resulted in a desired result for his customers, these "wins" were achieved through undesirable actions. Moreover, he was staffed in an open space environment and all of his coworkers and supervisor could hear his heated phone arguments. George admitted that on more than one occasion per week, he found himself slamming the phone down in frustration, which resulted in awkward smiles or laughs from his coworkers. As an individual contributor, he was a high performer who delivered great results, but he was not viewed as a potential leader because of his lack of emotional control.

After our first conversations, I realized that I would need to illustrate exactly how his lack of emotional intelligence was the sole reason he was being overlooked and how it was the basis of his boss' unwillingness to support him for promotion. The negative behavior was also having an impact on his stress level and his effectiveness with other clients. First, I had him take an emotional intelligence quiz as well as a "derailer" quiz. Remember, derailers are things that take you off the track toward your goals. He found out that he was not as emotionally intelligent as he thought he was, and he discovered the derailers that cause him to lose control. Once we discovered the areas of deficiency, I probed further to discover that many of these triggers resulted from childhood incidents. His father died at a very young age, and he was left to take care of his mother and sisters. Being the only man in the house, he constantly felt it was his job to defend his family and himself. George was always ready for a fight. He had transferred all of that brutish conduct to the workplace and—although he was skillfully defending the interests of his customers—the way in which he was doing it was effectively disqualifying him from furthering his career. The little boy trying to be a man was still showing up for the fight, and he didn't have the tools to fight correctly.

The quiz and our evaluation of the results helped George to look at his behavior differently. With the problem identified, it was time to put some tools into practice. I asked him to describe what usually happened when he felt the need to fight or when his blood pressure rose. He said his right leg began to tap rapidly, or he'd begin tapping something with his pen. I then asked what feelings he was having. *Was he feeling insulted, frustrated, angered, etc. when he started to exhibit this behavior?* Those were his triggers—tangible actions and emotions where he could identify when he was going from being productive to being unproductive. Those types of outward physical signs let him know that the little boy trying to be a man was about to show up and the adult man with better skills was fading away.

I had him read *The Four Agreements,* and we discussed not taking the third party representatives' actions personally. He or she was doing their job for their clients just as he was. Now that he had a heightened self-awareness, he could improve his self-management and his social awareness, which ultimately meant doing a better job with relationship management. I had him print out the actual four agreements on a card to keep at his desk so when the triggers came up, he had a visual reminder that he needed to stop and manage his emotions better. We also identified that there was an area nearby that he could go to in order to calm down and give himself the opportunity to respond effectively to the situation in control of his emotions. The third thing I suggested was that in instances when none of it worked, and he found himself reverting to the aggressive behavior that he stop and take five deep breaths (or as many as he needed to calm down) and visualize the desired outcome. At the end of the day when he had an instance that didn't turn out the way he wanted, or if he didn't get the results he wanted, he needed to take a moment to reflect on it. By visualizing what he could have done differently he was proactively correcting himself for the next time a similar incident occurred so that he could respond with the desired results.

We worked on this for a while, and when George started getting positive feedback from his coworkers, it served as a good reinforcement for the effort he was putting forth to improve his EQ. In time, his boss started noticing and praising the positive change. The full emotional intelligence evaluation was effective in making him much more aware. It gave him tools that allowed him to manage his emotions in an ideal way. So much so that the same boss who said he would never consider him for a promotion, recently promoted him.

SUMMARY

1. Self-awareness is the bedrock of emotional intelligence. If you first don't realize what you're doing and why you're doing it, you'll never be able to control it. It is different from self-criticism because it allows you to *understand* who you are and your opportunities for growth.

2. The foundation of self-management is bringing down the emotion and bringing up thinking by understanding when you have been triggered and looking for other, better options to accomplish your objective. That is your primary focus in self-management. Self-management is applying self-control to the active participation in identifying the best options for you to reach your objective or goals.

3. Social awareness is focused on developing empathy for others' goals and positions.

4. Relationship management is looking for the win-win in every situation and thinking *"and"* vs. *"or."* It is the last element because it is the consideration of how you leverage the first three competencies to make sure you're not only meeting your objectives, but you're also building solid relationships and influencing others. You are empowering the other person by acknowledging the value and validity of their point of view.

EXERCISE

Self-assessment: Emotional Intelligence. Now it is time for you to officially assess your EQ. There are numerous online quizzes you can take or you can work with a coach to start your EQ journey. The key is to remember to be honest when you are answering the questions. There are no right or wrong answers. This is about you and your development. Remember, the purpose of the quiz is to help you develop a road map to increasing your EQ. Here are a couple of free online quizzes:

- https://www.mindtools.com/pages/article/ei-quiz.htm
- http://globalleadershipfoundation.com/geit/eitest.html

CHAPTER 3

Improving Your Performance & Maximizing Your EQ

———————◆———————

Now that we're clear as to the four key competencies of emotional intelligence, let's apply some practical ways in which you can exercise your emotional intelligence on a day-to-day basis. I've done research and have read countless books on emotional intelligence and improving performance, and even for someone who enjoys the discussion, it can seem like a lot at times. I want to present things in a digestible way that can be used in the moment. Let's be honest, the majority of the times when you will need your EQ are times when you will be caught off guard or thrust into a situation. As I said, I want to give you access to information and tools you can use to change your situation and to improve your outcomes.

Below you will find my Four-Point Checklist to Exercising Emotional Intelligence. Each of the points provides a step-by-step way in which you can manage a situation and begin to heighten your emotional intelligence so that you respond rather than react. As you continue to use the checklist, it will become more intuitive and you will be able to execute it naturally and seamlessly. Until then, use it as a guide, a cheat sheet if you will, to help you increase your strengths and find opportunities for growth.

Four Steps to Exercising Emotional Intelligence

1. The first step is to understand and recognize when you hit a trigger or when something happens that causes you to hit a trigger. It is demonstrating self-awareness of the factors that make you react negatively to a person or a situation. A trigger is something that activates your amygdala and creates a feeling of fight-or-flight. Your triggers can include feeling attacked, bullied, embarrassed, or disrespected. Triggers can also include thinking another person is lazy or incompetent. Finally, triggers can be moral barometers when you feel someone is being dishonest or that a situation is unfair/unjust. For most people, triggers are accompanied by a physical manifestation, such as an eye twitch, a pen tap, a change in the tone of your voice, or even silence. All of these are examples of the various triggers that stand alone or work in concert to let you know that you have the potential to lose your EQ. It is imperative that when triggers begin, you notice them and understand that you are about to give the other person control. This is when it's time to engage the key competencies of emotional intelligence.

   My main triggers are incompetence, dishonesty, and bullying. I feel the little vein in my neck start to pulsate and then my voice starts to rise. It signals to me that I am starting to take something personally, which means I'm getting off track. At that point, I am no longer focused on my objective. I know it's time to pause. It's time to do an audit of the situation and engage my emotional intelligence by activating my prefrontal cortex.

   In order to activate your prefrontal cortex and stay in control of the situation, you must remember not to take another person's actions personally. It is always about their goals, objectives, and background. Once you are able to remember that it's not personal, you are more likely to be able to control your emotions and look at the big picture. It's not easy all the time, but it makes a big difference when you maintain control and focus on what is essential. I find that repeating the mantra, "this is not personal" to myself is a very effective calming mechanism that helps me focus on my objectives. Put a copy of the list of the actual four agreements from *The Four Agreements* book on your phone, at your desk, or on your bathroom mirror as a visual reminder that you should never take anything personally. It works for me.

2. The second step is to evaluate the questions you are asking yourself (keeping your prefrontal cortex active). We have to be careful of the stories we tell ourselves. Our questions lead to our actions, as is thoroughly outlined in the book *Change Your Questions, Change Your Life* by Marilee Adams. Oftentimes, our initial questions are not productive and can create negative emotions. We've all had that internal dialogue that makes matters worse. Those questions never lead to productive answers internally or productive action externally. Instead, they usually manifest in visible, physical reactions to the thoughts running through your head, which limit your options and impact. Once you change the questions, you change your response to the situation. Instead of asking those questions, try shifting the focus to making a positive impact. *How do I maintain control in this situation? What is my true objective? What is the takeaway from what this person is saying? What can I do to get back on track?* By moving from judgment to looking for ways to be productive, you move the situation into a partnership space. You will be surprised at the options that come to mind when you change your questions. It feels better when you have options, and you reach better outcomes, too.

3. Once you arrive in a partnership space, your sole job is to be an active listener. Not only does it allow you to hear the other person's perspective, it also allows you time to fully exercise self-management while you build your social awareness. Understanding the

other person's position is essential for you to be able to pinpoint opportunities for agreement and to reach a mutual objective. Listening eighty percent of the time and only talking for twenty percent of the time is the only way to truly understand another person's point of view and to identify opportunities. You don't have to agree. The goal is to understand and leverage what you understand in order to drive an appropriate outcome.

4. Next, you need to look for the win-win by thinking *and* instead of *or* in the moment. In the book, *Crucial Conversations* by Patterson, Grenny, McMillan & Switzler, they state that *and* questions solve problems as well as build relationships. For example, instead of asking, "How do I get them to understand the risks of their proposal?" change it to, "How do I present my concerns with the proposal and ensure that my peers feel safe and respected?" There is rarely a situation when one side is completely right and the other is completely wrong, or when there is no common ground where the two parties can meet and agree. Being empathetic to their needs and goals will give rise to options that keep you both on track toward your objectives.

It is extremely beneficial to be proactive as well. Naturally, there will be situations that will catch you off guard. Most of the time, you can anticipate when a meeting, conversation, or activity will give rise to a contentious moment. If you know that you're going into a meeting where there's a gap in perception, or you're going to meet with someone who is challenging, preparedness is your best defense. Setting your focus beforehand keeps your objectives clear and reduces the risk of activating your triggers. Decide on the best way to approach the meeting by focusing on adding value, finding opportunities, and getting to your objective. This approach cuts a potentially negative situation off head-on before one even arises.

As an example, George recently presented a problem to me regarding one of the employees he was newly supervising. He'd inherited this employee when he stepped into his new role, and the employee was notoriously late on assignments. George was frustrated to the point that he had stopped talking to the young lady altogether and had begun finishing the assignments himself. George had learned to control himself, but this employee was forcing him to take his relationship management to the next level as a supervisor.

George identified that many of his triggers were being activated during his interactions with this particular employee. In this employee, George disliked her lack of urgency, her level of incompetence, and her poor work ethic. As George relayed the story to me, I cautioned him not to be judgmental. Our judgment of others allows us to justify our behavior. With that considered—and based on the feedback from the employee's previous supervisor—he knew that this was not a problem unique to him, so he was able to not take her behavior and performance personally. He then took a night to evaluate the questions he was asking himself about this woman. He went from, "Why is she so incompetent?" to "What can I do to support her and make sure we achieve our group's objectives?" He clearly defined the objective of ensuring the team met its goal and helped her become more productive.

The next day George sat down with the employee to help develop a plan for improvement. In that meeting, he took the time to listen to the employee's issues surrounding the work and why she wasn't delivering on time. He did so without judgment, but instead he looked for ways to help her make an adjustment so that she could meet the production goals. In doing so, he discovered that the employee was really committed to doing a good job, but she was feeling overwhelmed. He also learned that the employee did not have an efficient process for getting the work done in a timely manner, which led to the overwhelmed feelings. The truth was, the employee felt inadequate and those feelings of failure further contributed to her inability to perform. She had not asked for help out of fear of looking incompetent, and no one had offered her assistance or support. George took ownership of finding ways to support her by developing a plan and helping her develop a better process. Together, they closed all the assignments that had been open for nearly two months. Now, the employee is on top of her deadlines, reports to work on time, and has a new level of engagement. By going through the steps outlined above, George impressed his manager by figuring out ways to help an employee who was widely seen as a problem.

Day-to-Day Application of Your Elevated EQ

How am I going to exercise my EQ today? Essentially, it is about being in the moment. None of this means anything if you only read it, understand it, and then don't use it. I recently had to take a step back and remember to apply it in a situation myself. The truth is, even once you've practiced this over and over again for years, there will be certain times or people that will push your buttons in ways that cause you to react unintelligently. The trick is to practice so much that even when you're outside of your desired self, it doesn't last to the point that you become ineffective. You will reach a point when you start to recognize that you are off or have allowed someone to take control of your behavior; that is growth. The key is to be aware, not perfect! Having awareness gives you an opportunity to make better decisions next time or to rectify the situation now by looking at different options. At that point, you are ahead of ninety percent of other people.

I will share a recent personal example. I was on a conference call about a very sensitive subject, and I didn't agree with the approach that was being suggested. On the call were members of our US team, and our global counterparts and we were on the opposite ends of the spectrum on the issue. One of the senior level executives, who is from France, said, "I'm from France, so I am a very straight shooter so I'm just going to say it." She then proceeded to say something that I felt was inappropriate and downright inaccurate. I felt attacked, disrespected, and that the information was wrong. Before I knew it, I was in an amygdala hijacking and the vein in my neck was throbbing. I replied, "Well, I appreciate you being a straight shooter, I am too." And I shot right back at her.

As soon as the shots were fired, I knew that I'd crossed the line. I had taken what she said personally and reacted to her aggression with aggression. My ego took over the conversation, and I lost control of my emotions. Thankfully, I was able to stop and assess my actions by asking myself those questions: 1) What is my real objective here? 2) What am I afraid of? 3) What am I feeling? 4) How I do get this conversation back on track? and, 5) What is the win-win? I began to look for ways to get the conversation back on track. My goal switched from one-upping her to finding a way to have a civil conversation and reach an agreement, and ways in which we could develop an action plan together that satisfied both of our objectives.

The best way for me to regain control of the conversation was to become empathetic to her position by asking questions. "I understand your position, are there any other options that have been evaluated? Is it possible for us to look at all the options? What do you think about us working to come up with at least four options to evaluate and present to the committee with our final recommendation?" By the end of the conversation we had collectively identified and agreed upon an entirely different option than either one of us had proposed. By taking a pause and going through the steps, I was able to change course and prevent what would have undoubtedly been a verbal brawl. She was a straight shooter and so was I. The difference was I saw the opportunity to stop and apply emotional intelligence to the situation. By using my social awareness skills, I realized that because of her position in the organization, she had the great majority of people on her side. I was not going to win by being combative with her, and we would have ended up with what I thought was a subpar recommendation. I certainly was not going to achieve my objective, and it was only going to make me look very bad on this global call.

When you can be in the moment by recognizing that you've turned your emotional intelligence off, you can stop and use the different tools you have from the four competencies. Now, there will be times when you come up against a bully who will not relent. There is a bully in every organization (just make sure it's not you). In those instances, it doesn't matter if you go through three steps or thirty-five; it is a situation that is not going to end well. The emotionally intelligent thing to do is to stop the conversation. Acknowledge that the subject is important to the other person and request to revisit at another time or offline. Basically, you're stopping the conversation rather than proceed in the same energy that was not going end with your objective. And if that doesn't work, then it may be necessary to escalate the issue up the chain of command. Find a mediator or someone else who can help you and the other person find common ground. Again, that shows leadership from your perspective and exhibits emotional intelligence.

We talked about journaling earlier and you had the chance to practice. Keeping a daily journal of instances when I was successful, and more importantly, instances when there was an opportunity for growth is a great way to improve your EQ. I do it at the end of the day, especially when I have had a situation (whether it is work or personal) that didn't go the way I wanted. I do a reflection, and I have my coaching clients do the same thing. The questions to ask are:

1. What would be the ideal outcome in that situation?
2. What could I have done differently to achieve that outcome?
3. What can I do tomorrow to address that situation more effectively?
4. What can I do in the future when I encounter a similar situation?

This restarts you and it prepares you for the future. It is exercising and perfecting your emotional intelligence muscles. It also takes you out of frustration or playing the victim or beating yourself up about a mistake. We all make mistakes, but high potential achievers learn from their mistakes. Taking the time to journal is a key component of your EQ because it allows you to be self and socially aware. From there you can identify what you are going to do moving forward in this situation or a future situation that is similar while engaging the other components. One of my key mantras is that you have an opportunity every day to be better than you were the day before. But, the only way you can be better is if you recognize what went wrong the previous day.

> Every day, you have an opportunity to be better than you were the day before.

SUMMARY

1. Utilize the four steps to maximize your EQ.

2. Probative questions will help you identify another person's goals while you look for the win-win solution.

3. Sometimes the best thing to do is stop the conversation so everyone can regroup, especially when dealing with a bully.

4. Keep a daily journal of your EQ success and growth opportunities.

EXERCISE

For one week, keep a daily journal of your interactions and how you effectively exercised your EQ. At the end of the day, think back to situations (work and/or personal) that went well and those that didn't go the way you wanted. Break down each by the four key competencies (Self-Awareness, Self-Management, Social Awareness, and Relationship Management) and assess where your strengths were and where there were growth opportunities. This exercise will help strengthen your EQ and prepare you to respond versus react more consistently. Try it for one week straight and you will notice a significant difference. I must warn you to be patient with yourself. Remember this is not about being perfect—it's about being aware and growing. You will have hiccups, but the difference between you and the average person is that you will recognize the hiccup and have the tools to make better decisions in the future.

SECTION II—PERCEPTIONS

PERCEPTION
DEFINITION
THE WAY IN WHICH SOMETHING IS REGARDED, UNDERSTOOD, OR INTERPRETED

SOURCE: BUSINESSDICTIONARY.COM

How you are perceived in business is directly related to how success-ful you become. Perceptions drive the opportunities you receive—the promotions, assignments, and so on. You can be the hardest work-ing, most loyal, and thoughtful employee in the organization and it will make no difference if that is not what others perceive you to be. Conversely, I have seen a person succeed primarily on the strength of how they were "regarded, understood, or interpreted." Perception is the translation of the stimuli and information we take in through the five senses; we then interpret that into a judgment of a person or situation. In addition to our five senses, we also translate how someone makes us feel into a perception.

> "I've learned that people will forget what you said, people will forget what you did, but people will never forget how you made them feel."
>
> –Dr. Maya Angelou

A person develops a perception of you immediately, and then it evolves over time as your interactions increase. The good news is that you can drive the perceptions people have about you. A mistake many people make is that they never learn what the prevailing perceptions are about them. In this section, we will discuss branding and how packaging and confidence impact your brand, and ultimately, the perceptions people have about you. Whether you know it or not, you have a brand and it is either helping you or hurting you.

First let's do a quick overview of the different stages of the perceptual process that everyone goes through about others and themselves. The different stages are:

1. **Receiving**: It can be argued that this first stage in the process is the most important. Receiving is the stage that we collect information via all of our senses. In business, first

impressions mean everything. It is far more difficult to improve your perception in someone's eyes after making a bad first impression.

2. **Selecting**: After a person receives the initial information, they begin to select what information they receive in accordance with their interest, needs, or desires. Selection is controlled by both internal and external factors.

    a. Internal: A person's background, education, psychological state, experience, self-awareness, self-acceptance, and personal goals all play a role in how you are perceived by them.

    b. External: The factors are intensity, size, contrast, movement, repetition, familiarity, and novelty.

3. **Organizing**: Next, we all organize the information and stimuli received in categories that dictate the way we interact with someone else. A person whose information arouses our senses in a positive way is perceived differently and our interactions are positively affected. The opposite is also true.

4. **Interpreting:** Finally, we all use everything gathered in the previous three stages to form an idea about someone. We interpret the information we've received to formulate an opinion by giving meaning and categorizing. This stage includes, stereotyping, the halo effect, and other perceptions that we will discuss.

Before being concerned about how others perceive you, you must first determine how you perceive yourself. Oftentimes, you may wish to modify your personal perception to match how you would like to be perceived by others.

CHAPTER 4

Are You a Hyundai or a Bentley?

————◆————

Coca-Cola®, Microsoft®, Citibank®, and Apple® are all household name brands of products and services. The name alone signifies a response in all of our minds that is associated with the companies' reputation in the marketplace. Each of these companies has successfully branded itself for that very reason. It's easy to understand branding when you think about it in the context of a global company that sells goods or services, but branding is just as important for you. Similarly, when someone mentions your name, the thoughts evoked are crucial to your success in the workplace and beyond. Your brand is the key driver of the *Perceptions* people have about you. You want to be in control of defining your brand, and not let anyone else define it for you. Another way to look at branding is the story you want told by your work, presentation, and reputation. Your brand is the cornerstone of your personal story that will affect how people treat you and the reaches of your success.

"All of us need to understand the importance of branding. We are CEOs of our own companies: Me, Inc. To be in business today, our most important job is to be head marketer for the brand called You."

—Tom Peters

Building and managing your corporate and personal brand is important whether you are an accountant, an actor, or a CEO. Why? Because ninety percent of the decisions made about you and your career are made while you're not in the room. Think about it. Your annual review, a bonus or pay increase, a promotion, a hiring decision, a lay-off, a casted role, a new contract, a new assignment, and so on are all decisions that are made about you and your professional future without you in the room. They are decisions made based on how others have perceived you. More than likely, you won't have a team of marketers, publicists, and branding specialists working with you like the above-mentioned brands, but you still need to spend time thinking about the snapshots and perceptions that people have of you. This includes everything from the way you engage in meetings to the types of questions you ask to the package (the totality of your being) you show up with, which is extremely important as far as credibility is concerned. I've seen people who are exceptionally competent with great ideas be discounted merely because of the package and the way they show up at work. Another component in a corporate setting is evaluating the priorities and practices of the organization to ensure that your brand is aligned with those imperatives while also remaining authentic and true to whom you are as an individual.

I often receive a bit of pushback when we start talking about branding. In today's society, there are so many people talking about it that I think it gets a bit distorted. True, there are many tools that public and private figures use to define their brands—social media, blogs, and websites, are all mechanisms in which celebrities, entrepreneurs, and professionals use to define and further expand the reach of their brands. But what if you're not a Kardashian (where your name itself is a built-in brand, for good or bad) or the next singing sensation? You still need to work on your branding. In the first part of this book, I established my brand by sharing my credentials and background. Branding builds credibility. If I had told you I have been stuck in the same dead-end job for ten years or unemployed unable to find a job for five years, you would not have perceived me as a credible source for career advice.

Most people would say, "I am not a brand. I am a person." Well, that's true to an extent. However, whether you like it or not, you're always in the business of selling a product. The product just so happens to be *you!* Your brand attracts employers, spouses, friends, and so on. In all these situations, you're selling your abilities, ideas, and qualities. I know some of it may not feel right to some you, but it's the truth if you take some time to think about it. The more you think of yourself as a brand, the better salesperson you will become. Since it is happening anyway, you might as well control the messaging so that you leave people with what you want. For example, we've discussed emotional intelligence at length. Part of your brand could be that you're overly emotional, not communicative, or difficult to work with on projects. These are all things that could be a part of your brand that can limit you. But you have the power to change the narrative and conversation by putting some thought and effort into defining your brand yourself. Basically, when I think of your professional brand I am asking the following questions:

1. What are you known for?

2. What do people say or think when your name is mentioned?

3. What are your strengths?

4. What are your areas of opportunity?

The answers to these questions make up your brand; smart people adjust the negative and maximize the positive of their branding. You have a brand whether you know it or not, but what you really want to do is be in control of it and manage the ways in which you are perceived.

Oprah Winfrey has by far one of the best professional and personal brands today. Over the course of thirty or so years, she has been clear that she wanted to be perceived as a vessel and teacher for you to live your best life. Her name and companies are synonymous with excellence and the best of humanity. Oprah's brand goes beyond her own success with its ability to elevate other brands by mere association. When Oprah says that a book is worth reading (hint to Oprah) millions of people read it. "Oprah's Favorite Things" guarantees record sales for consumer brands and products. And if she says a person is worth listening to, that person becomes Dr. Phil, Rachel Ray, or Iyanla Vanzant. Oprah is the quintessential model for an excellent, well thought out brand that is universally perceived as positive and authentic.

Donald Trump is also a perfect example in the opposite manner. Prior to his run for President (or, maybe before he attacked President Obama) he was widely known as a billionaire real estate mogul and brazen reality star of *The Apprentice*. Politics and personal opinions aside, most people did not challenge that he was a successful businessman. He then decided to run for President and that all began to change. True, he ultimately became the President; however, his personal and professional brand took a devastating hit.

The Trump name used to mean the best in luxury and lifestyle, allowing Trump and his family to license the name on everything from hotels to water. Now, there is a large group of people who believe that the Trump name means something entirely different and the brand is steadily declining in the way it is perceived. Independent of which side of the political aisle you stand on, there is no denying that the perception of what the Trump brand stands for is much more negative than it ever was before he ran for President.

My process of getting to my brand was not an overnight thing as there are many layers to it. As far as my personal brand role models go, "Aunt" Doris Carter was definitely one for me. She was always professional, prepared, and organized. A big part of her brand was people and investing in them—not only investing to help her business, but in an effort to help them as people. You knew if Doris Carter was involved in a project—whether it involved one of her employees, a neighbor, or a patient—people were going to receive help and assistance. Looking back on it, it was clear to everyone that her brand was professionalism and service.

In fact, professionalism is the main thing that I remember Aunt Doris driving home with me. She insisted that I be professional no matter what was going on—from my dress; to the way I spoke, to my overall preparation. Particularly, she would stress that professionalism meant that when I didn't know something, I was confident in saying that I didn't know it, but I also had to have a plan to find out. She was grooming me to be a responsible and responsive teammate and leader. I remember that this was most apparent when things weren't going well with the business. She would ask me questions like, "As a leader and knowing that this [negative] thing is going on, what do you do to instill confidence in the people who are reporting to you?" She'd wait for me to come up with a solution and then help me steer back on track when I was coming up short.

Aunt Doris taught me a great deal about how to manage through challenges or difficult situations by first being honest, but also by using forward-thinking to find a solution and appropriate next step. I always had to have a plan, and this comforted her. Even if it was not fully fleshed out, there was something to move toward, which gave her confidence in me and allowed others to follow my lead.

Let's be clear, I wasn't always on top of it. There were times when I didn't show up big in a situation, namely if I came to a meeting with her disorganized. I can hear her saying it now, "I don't have time for you to come here and get organized. You need to show up organized. Obviously, I wasn't important enough for you to do it before you got here. Come back when you are prepared to meet with me." She was setting an expectation of excellence with me. Aunt Doris did not play games and I am a better professional and person for it.

The lessons I learned from Aunt Doris have helped me countless times throughout my career as I worked to define my professional brand. One specific example was a story I've previously shared about how I was presenting myself in meetings. I received feedback from my manager that I was not showing up big when it counted. While I had all these great ideas and I was producing results in my role, I wasn't saying anything when the opportunity presented itself in front of senior leadership. I was missing a branding opportunity.

For some people, defining their brand comes easily while others find it a bit more difficult. For me, it evolved over the years and I have been able to refine my professional brand with a focus on the next levels of my career. The key is that I had to ensure it was authentic to who I am. My corporate brand is an inspirational-leader, strategic-thinker, and people-developer. Once I was able to identify the adjectives that described the goals of my brand, aligning my package and my actions made it easier to manage the brand from that lens.

Now, I didn't go around saying, "Hey, I am an inspirational, strategic, people developer." That would be ineffective. Instead, I took an account of everything I was doing and whether it was in line with my brand definition and my authentic self. I made an assessment of my actions to make sure that was the new narrative for who I am professionally. With the narrative defined in words, I could then begin to manage my actions accordingly and position myself for opportunities to demonstrate the characteristics. By defining my brand and understanding why each component was important, I had a clear target to work towards instead of waiting to see how people perceived me. I started working intentionally to frame the narrative. I had to make sure that I was inspiring people on my team and colleagues outside of my team. I had to make sure I was demonstrating strategic thinking, problem solving, and effective execution. I started sharing more about my investment in people development at work and in the community, highlighting my work at the Hope Academy in Newark, my girls, and my work as Chairman of the Board of Sunshine's Open-Door Foundation. I think the same is true for your personal brand. It's about deciding what you want people to say about you when you're not in the room and adjusting your actions accordingly.

So, where do you start? The first component you should evaluate is your current brand by assessing how you show up at work and in rooms of importance. A good way to gauge where you are is to look to the people that are in the types of positions that you aspire to and assess how they are presenting themselves. It's a great place to start. Then evaluate how you presently measure up to them. The most effective way to do this is to ask yourself a series of questions and answer them as honestly as you can. Be truthful without being brutal because beating yourself up is ineffective in getting to a place of opportunity. It's all about growth and excelling to the next level of your career. Here are some helpful questions to get you started:

1. How do you show up? Evaluate everything from your wardrobe choices, your hairstyle, how you articulate, how you walk into a room, how you sit, etc. Look at all the components that you want to become a part of your overarching brand.

2. How much confidence do you exude when you go into a meeting? Are you sitting in the back with your head down or are you sitting upfront engaged?

3. Can you describe your *current* package in three adjectives? Do so, and then describe your *ideal* package with three adjectives. How do you change the way you show up to match your ideal package?

Once you have evaluated your present brand in relationship to your goals, you then must evaluate the qualities that are important to your environment/organization. If you're at a company where they appreciate innovative, creative people who think outside of the box, you determine how you can align your behavior with the organization's goals. Conversely, if you're in a more traditional organization that values conformity and predictability, then you either align yourself with their ideals or you might need to determine if you're in the right place. Either way or in every situation, you want to make sure that you're showing up a way that says, "I'm competent. I'm confident. I'm impactful, and I am in line with this organization's values."

With that said, none of it will work if you are not being authentic and true to who you are. Naturally, you can make some adjustments to blend into your environment, but you should not be making a complete overhaul of who you are and the things that you value. If you do, it won't work out and you won't be happy. You have to align with your authentic self and what is important to you. And if that does not align with the environment that you're presently in, then that's where I hope this book will help you. If you're feeling that you're in a place where you're not able to thrive or be your absolute best, you are in the wrong place. Asking these hard questions begins the process of discovering your purpose versus just living or earning or working. It's the next level mind-set and is also essential in defining your brand. Now, I'm not saying quit your job because you don't like an aspect of the culture or it is not one hundred percent aligned with you. What I'm offering you is a lens to evaluate what's important to you, and what is important to the organization to determine if there is alignment. If you are unaligned, the positioning section of this book will help you develop an exit plan.

I will share a quick story on how an organization's objectives impacted my branding strategy. At the time, I was a sales manager leading a team of sales specialist in the New York area. I had been a manager for a few years and I was frustrated that I was not being seriously considered for a marketing position despite being a consistent high performer and working with the marketing teams on a number of successful initiatives. I was in a one-on-one with one of my mentors who was an executive in the corporation, and I expressed my frustration. He asked me where I saw myself in the next three to five years and I told him as a head of marketing for a brand team. He replied; "Marion, marketing is perceived as the strategic arm of this organization. I am going to be honest with you, it will be tough for you to become a head of marketing in this organization for two reasons: one, you are in sales; and, two, you are African American. Neither are viewed as strategic in this company."

Now, my mentor was Caucasian. He was a good mentor and had great intentions. I was disappointed to hear his feedback and honestly a bit shocked. But when I looked around the organization; he was right. So, I started rattling off all the strategic things I had done and was currently doing that had led to my team's success as well as some of the brands I worked with on different initiatives. He told me, "it doesn't matter until they start associating you with strategic thinking."

I went to work to add strategic thinker into my three brand description adjectives. I knew I was very strategic, but as he said, it didn't matter until the powers that be in the organization thought so too. I started using the word strategy a lot more to describe how I had adjusted the brand plans to win big in my area. I started reading more books on strategy so I could speak the language more fluently and grow as a strategic thinker (*Decisive* by the Heath Brothers is a great book on strategic thinking). I started asking questions in meetings about "trip wires" (predetermined points of evaluation) to evaluate success of new initiatives, how we test the assumptions we were making as a company, and how the company's overall strategy could be executed in my department. Soon strategic thinker was a part of my core brand. Not only did I get into the marketing department, I eventually became the first African American man to become a head of marketing in one of the biggest companies in the world.

Self-evaluation is the essential first step because you have to be clear about what you think of yourself and your brand first. Following self-evaluation, it is equally important to understand how others perceive you. You should identify three to five people whom you trust to give honest and accurate feedback. You can simply ask them, "When I show up what do you see? Or, how do I show up in a room, at work, in meetings, or at home?" Ask your manager what they see as your strengths and areas of opportunity. Ask your family the same questions. The more people you survey, the greater representation you will receive because you will begin to see patterns in comments.

Or, you can do a 360 survey that will be inclusive of all the above (we discussed the benefit of my 360 feedback earlier). A 360 survey is a tool used by human resources (HR) professionals or executive coaches where you get feedback from people such as your direct reports, peers, your boss, and in some instances, your family. For a fee, the survey results will compile all the responses to identify patterns for you based on the type of survey you've selected and the questions asked.

A 360° survey is an effective tool to use in determining how you're presenting your brand and the areas of opportunity as identified from the people that are closest to you professionally and personally. You have to be prepared for the eye-opening feedback because I find that many times my clients see themselves one way while the rest of the world sees something totally differently. If you can afford to do one, the great thing about a 360 survey is that you can design it along with the help of your HR representative or executive coach to elicit the kinds of responses that are specific to you and your goals. You rank yourself in the areas and your answers are compared with those you've chosen to survey. It gives you a great and effective snapshot of how you are actually perceived.

You've self-assessed and you've received feedback from others. Now comes the hardest part of developing your brand—getting honest with how to move forward. You have to go back to the perceptions you would like for others to have about you and measure those against your present reality. Here is your opportunity to begin to define your brand according to your goals and what is important to you as well as your career. Within an organization, you need to understand what is also important for the role that you are striving for and the level you wish to attain. So, if you're trying to be the head of a strategy group and you're not looked at as being very strategic, you have some work to do. You now know your strengths and your areas of opportunity—one or two areas where you can enhance and improve the perceptions about your brand. Yet, just knowing these areas is futile if you don't implement it into your daily practice by going back to managing your self-awareness, understanding it, getting other people on board to help provide feedback, and staying diligent on a growth pathway. At that point, it is about the process of being aware and continuing to move forward.

We began this chapter by identifying some of the most famous product and service brands. Although it is helpful to use those brands to illustrate the power of effective branding, I also have never been a fan of thinking of myself as a Coke®. Yes, you are a product, but not in the same way as soda. Instead, I constructed a brand statement that is relevant to a human being. I support the idea of identifying how you'd like to be known. As I said, my professional brand goal is to be known as an inspirational, strategic, people-developer. That way, I am always self-assessing and managing my actions from that perspective. It also helps me to pinpoint the resources I have available to me that help craft that brand and tell that story more effectively. This helps me to get other people to tell that story about me when I am not in the room.

SUMMARY

1. Ninety percent of the decisions that are made about you and your career are made when you are not in the room.

2. You want to be in control of defining your brand and not let anyone else define it for you. Another way to look at

branding is the story you want told about your work, presentation, and reputation.

3. Your brand is the cornerstone of your personal story that will affect the perceptions people have about you, and how successful you can become.

4. It is critical to understand your current brand, and identify the brand you would like to have by aligning your strengths and passions with the goals and objectives of the organization.

5. Cleary define the three adjectives you would like to be associated with your brand and drive that narrative through planning and action.

EXERCISE

1. Ask four people at work and three to four people in your personal life about your brand. Let them know you are working on your career plan and need their insights.

    Here are some questions to get you started:
    a. How do I show up in meetings? How do I show up at home?

    b. What are three adjectives you would use to describe me?

    c. How do I deal with problems?

    d. What would you say are my three strengths? What are my three areas of opportunity?

    e. If you had to describe me in one sentence, what would it be?

    Leave the questions open; do not try to explain what you mean. Ask them to answer the question the way they think best. Look for common themes between all the responses. This is your current brand!

2. Based on what you have learned and already know about yourself and the organization, identify the three adjectives you want
   to be associated with you and your brand.
3. Now take action to start driving the narrative around your
   desired brand.

CHAPTER 5

Do You Hear What You're Not Saying?

————◆————

Effective communication goes far beyond the actual words you speak or write. *The Business Dictionary* (http://www.businessdictionary.com/) has an elevated definition of effective communication, "A two-way information sharing process, which involves one party sending a message that is easily understood by the receiving party. Effective communication by business managers facilitates information sharing between company employees and can substantially contribute to its commercial success." I think it's far simpler than that—effective communication is choosing the best way to get your point across. The challenge is that we often believe that we are being clear in our messaging when in fact we are not or we are sending a completely different message. This is important because our verbal and nonverbal communication drives our brand and ultimately our perceptions.

> "The art of communication is the language of leadership."
>
> −James Humes

In my workshops, I ask participants to rank, by a percentage, which of the components of effective communication matter the most. The three components are:

1) The actual content (or words) spoken;

2) The tone of voice (accent, emphasis, excitement, powerful pauses); and,

3) Appearance and body language (visual).

A study by Professor Albert Mehrabian of the University of California in Los Angeles assigned fifty-five percent, thirty-eight percent, or seven percent (55%, 38%, or 7% respectively) to the level of importance of each of these three components on how effectively your message is received. I ask participants to assign where they think each percentage goes with respect to the three components. Invariably, most people assign the greatest percentage, fifty-five percent to the first component—the actual content—with the tone of voice and non-verbal communication swapping between the thirty-eight percent and seven percent depending on the group. According to the studies, however, it's quite different. Your appearance and body language account for fifty-five percent of the pie graph while your tone of voice makes up thirty-eight percent, and the actual words you say are the least important with seven percent according to countless studies on effective communication.

MEHRABIAN'S RULE OF PERSONAL COMMUNICATION

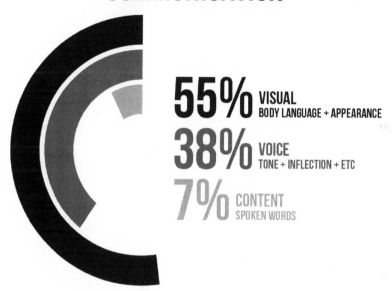

55% VISUAL
BODY LANGUAGE + APPEARANCE

38% VOICE
TONE + INFLECTION + ETC

7% CONTENT
SPOKEN WORDS

Over my career I have found this breakdown to hold true for how people perceive me and how I perceive others. There is an abundance of research that shows that judgments are made within the first seven seconds of you engaging with someone and you have a whopping five to seven seconds to confirm or change people's perceptions about you. Naturally, if your appearance and body language are communicating the wrong message, you will be starting at a deficit with your audience that will be very difficult to overcome even if your delivery and content are spectacular.

Similar to performance, good content is the price of entry. More than likely, you would not be in the room if you didn't have something of value to add content-wise. Now, the real goal is to get people to receive your content, and more importantly, believe it so they buy into it. The reason so many groups get the percentages wrong is that the majority of people concentrate all their energy on developing the content for a presentation. As we have discussed throughout the book (and in the last chapter), your content can be amazing, but if the way in which you're showing up is not aligned with the quality of the content, then the content won't matter. The pie chart and percentages allow us to quantify the importance of everything other than the content and drive this point home. As with most things, the equation is not an absolute. It is merely a tool to illustrate the importance of non-verbal communication on getting your point across to others and driving your perceptions and how you are perceived by them. Obviously, there are other factors at play in every situation that will affect how your message is received.

The great news is that you can prepare for the non-verbal communication as well as you do the verbal parts. First, you can make sure your appearance matches your message (more about that later in the section on packaging).

I can't stress enough how important non-verbal communication coupled with effective verbal communication is to establishing and refining your brand. Where you choose to sit in a room, the level of engagement you demonstrate (leaning forward, taking notes, etc.), and the type of questions you ask all play an integral role in how you are perceived by your peers and management. Those little things make a big difference, which is why I keep repeating their importance. You could be writing a note that says, "Old MacDonald had a farm," but it looks like you're taking notes based on the content of the meeting. Do everything you can do to make sure it is understood that you are engaged and present for whatever is going on in the meeting. Never underestimate the power of a great question that not only shows engagement, but also gets the presenter and the other participants to think. A question that adds insight to a meeting and has the potential to generate a productive conversation that leads to something valuable is always a great way to infuse your brand into a meeting.

You Are Being Judged By Your Cover

Now let's go deeper into a critical component of nonverbal communication that impacts your branding—your packaging. The ugly truth is we are all books being judged by our covers. As Whitney Houston said, "It's not right, but it's okay." It's okay because we have control over how we show up. The challenge is too many people discount this important aspect of branding.

As stated earlier, fifty-five percent of how you are received by others is focused on your appearance and body language. Think of packaging as a vessel to get your message heard. Your package is everything from the outfit you're wearing, the fit of what you're wearing, the way you wear your hair, the jewelry you are wearing, and your overall grooming. Your package is critical because as I previously stated; within the first seven seconds, people make a judgment about you, your value, and your credibility before you say a word. If you come in and you have a bad package, you're starting from a deficit position. Now you have put yourself in the position where you have to be flawless and can't have any mistakes or show nervousness because you have to dig yourself out of a negative hole. However, if you come in with a very positive package, then you have what is called a positive halo effect. You have instant credibility and now you just have to deliver on that credibility. There's a huge difference in how you are received and what you must do from there on to either retain or gain credibility. The overarching idea is the same for men and women—your appearance needs to be crisp, clean, appropriate, and fit the environment.

Formulas aside, if we apply common sense to this we know that it is the truth. We have all been in meetings, seminars, and/or conferences where we've stopped listening before someone was able to deliver their content because of the way they were dressed or poor body language. It's how our society is and Corporate America is just a microcosm of the greater society. The better dressed you are, the more people are interested and willing to engage with you.

For example, let's say you are searching for a new luxury car and you go into a car dealership. There are two sales people standing there greeting you as you enter. One salesperson has on a tailored suit, nice glasses, and polished shoes. The other salesperson has on jeans with holes in them, an ill fitted shirt, and a bad haircut. Which one do you want to help you pick out your new luxury vehicle?

Early on, my packaging helped me a great deal in creating my personal brand perceptions within and outside of my respective organizations. I know that I receive a lot of instant credibility solely based on what I am wearing. As superficial as it sounds (and may be), it is the reality that we are more often than not judged by our appearance. It isn't something that is going to change any time soon, if ever, so make it a positive indicator for you. My dad was the one who instilled this in me—always be the best-dressed guy in the room. He believed that you could be dead broke, but when you show up looking like you're worth a million bucks, people will treat you like you're worth a million bucks. His advice always resonated with me and you already know that I come from humble beginnings. Even still, I always worked to show up in a manner that represented the place I wanted to be and not necessarily where I was. That's why many people who knew me when I was growing up will be surprised to read how much we struggled financially when I was a kid. We were broke, but you couldn't tell it when we left the house.

Early in my career, I was a part of a team that was scheduled to do a big presentation. The team leader of the presentation was very strong. She looked amazing, was very sharp in the way she spoke, and her style was expertly polished. She engaged the audience from the moment she stepped up to speak solely from her appearance.

Then, another member of our team who had brilliant content took the stage. He was also an expert in his area, but his package did not match his expertise. His pants were too long, his shirt was baggy and stained from lunch, and his shoes were scuffed and in desperate need of a polish. Overall, he just didn't look the part of a credible resource for this audience of two hundred people. To make things worse, he also showed visible signs of nervousness by beginning to cough, shuffle his papers, and ramble during his presentation. He was doomed from the outset.

Based on his package and how he showed up, people became distracted. Our audience began to check their phones, talk, and take "bathroom" breaks. You could see a marked difference in the level of engagement from the audience from when the lead presented. He had very valuable and insightful content, and if the audience had listened to him, they would have taken away some really powerful tools. Thankfully, the next member of the team who took the stage had a great package and was able to re-engage the audience. So, even though the previous guy had the most innovative and impactful content, it wasn't received.

I use this example when I am presenting to young people to demonstrate the importance of presentation as your first means of communication in everyday life. The students tend to understand it right away. Since no one was listening to him, it didn't matter how much time he spent on creating amazing content. After all of his hard work preparing the message, no one was listening and none of his great ideas were heard. There was no real value added because no one paid attention.

The same is true for our daily interactions—the first way we communicate is how we present ourselves. And it's not just a great lesson for young people, it is extremely important in a corporate setting. The way you present yourself is how you get people's attention. It's how you get them to listen to and respect what you're trying to say. Granted, it is unfortunate that we judge each other that way, but again it's the way of the world.

I am not saying you can't overcome the initial impressions, because you can. However, with a strong package, they're going to give you more leeway because the perception from your package is, "this person is credible and has something of value to communicate." Conversely, if it's all show and no substance, then you will lose your audience once they discover their perceptions based on your package were inaccurate. A great package gets you in the door and provides that positive halo effect. It also has direct relationship to you achieving your goal of impactful communication. That way, people actually receive the message that you're trying to deliver.

You need to be sure that you are representing where you want to be and not where you are. Your packaging should represent your aspirations versus your current situation. You should be presenting yourself at the next level of your career. People want to be promoted to the next level, but they're showing up demonstrating (from a visual perspective) that they are not ready for it. Look to the people that are at the level to which you aspire and match them in presentation. It communicates that you're already prepared for the next level without you ever saying a word.

I mentored a young man some years ago that had been with the company for two years, but he was extremely frustrated because he wasn't being considered for the roles he applied for and wanted. He received feedback that he was competent, however, he still was not being promoted, so he came to me for help. I evaluated his performance, read his reviews, observed him in some meetings, and determined that it was his package that was holding him back. He came in every day looking as if he might be going to the gym after work. He could use a fresh haircut and when his clothes didn't resemble athletic gear, they were a bit too old and worn down. He was not dressing the part to match the roles that he aspired to have.

I had him pay attention to the men who were in the roles he wanted and those roles that were higher on the organizational chart to observe how they presented themselves. It wasn't about spending a lot of money. It was about getting the right wardrobe pieces for work that fit, matched each other, and were crisply maintained. He needed to be better groomed for people to take him seriously. It took about six months, but once he made the adjustment, he began to get recognized, and then eventually moved to a higher profile role that took him closer to his desired position. It also added to his confidence, which we will discuss later. In effect, he began communicating through his appearance that he was serious about the job and his future with the company.

Another example is one of my coaching clients who told me that she thought her package was fine and it was other factors that kept her from moving ahead. She was correct. She did dress fine for the job that she was doing at the time. She wasn't dressing for the job she desired. You have to start to prepare yourself mentally to go to that next level, including presenting the corresponding package. As a creative professional, she would come to work in a myriad of outfits that were appropriate for a creative environment. But she wanted to move into senior leadership, which was a different arena than the creative space. They dressed differently. She was going into meetings with the finance, marketing, and sales leaders with a package that was not aligning with the role she desired. Her package was not giving her the credibility to go to the next level in the minds of the people who mattered. She had to show up as a leader in the marketing department and not the creative space.

I asked her, "Could you represent your manager or department head at a next level meeting with what you wore to work today?" The answer was clear so she took the initiative to consult a grooming and styling service that designed a wardrobe based on her personality and her career goals. The service provides outfit suggestions and sends them to you; you have the choice of buying or not. Or, you can go to a department store and get free advice from their stylist (this goes for men and women).

Once she began to work with the service and changed her packaging, perceptions about her abilities within the organization began to change. She increased her credibility and was being heard more because people were taking her seriously. Her recommendations had greater impact on her team and throughout the organization. The key was that she wasn't dressing up, because that would have been inauthentic to her creative personality; she was just dressing differently. She was ultimately promoted and is now a senior level manager in the company. She didn't have to change who she was, she just had to adjust how she communicated her ability and goals through her package.

There are additional considerations to make in terms of the package you present at work. Many offices have adopted casual Fridays or casual summer policies to relax the burden of dressing up for work every day. There was this post on the internet about the "woman who ruined casual Fridays." She was a substantial woman wearing a halter top showing her cleavage and very short "Daisy Duke" shorts. The joke was that this woman killed casual Fridays; you don't want that to be you. Even on casual Fridays, you have to remember that you are still at work. An outfit may be fashionable, but it still may not be corporate attire.

If you wear a short-sleeved shirt, wear a short-sleeved shirt that has a collar on it. If you're going to wear jeans, make sure they are dark colored jeans with no holes or rips. And I know many people do this, but I advise against wearing sneakers to work, especially if you're trying to get promoted or move to the next level. My advice is always erring on the side of professionalism. You should always present a very strong-looking package no matter what the environment—whether it's casual Fridays or a business trip with colleagues. Your package should stand out as being extremely professional at all times.

SUMMARY

Here are some general tips for both men and women to remember:

- You are marketing a product—*Yourself.*

- First impressions are *Critical.* People judge you and your value in the first 7 seconds of seeing you.

- How you show up communicates who you are in the minds of others and it influences *Career Advancement.*

- *Appearance* influences perceptions, authority, intelligence, and suitability for hire or promotion. 93% of how your message is received is based on nonverbal communication.

EXERCISE

1. Evaluate someone who is perceived as polished and professional and who is at the level to which you aspire. Ask them for recommendations.

2. Go to the mall or a style consultant and tell them what you want to project in your package. Ask them for styling tips.

3. Test some mail order styling companies (it does not cost you anything unless you decide to keep the clothes). It's a great way to get ideas (Trunk Club and Stitch Fix are a couple you could start with).

Bonus Packaging Tips

Dressing for Success—Men

Granted, men have it a bit easier because we have fewer choices than women, particularly in a traditional corporate setting. Here are the three key considerations for men:

1. Fresh and clean. It is remarkable how many times I have been in interviews and meetings where a man has come in with either dirty or wrinkled clothes. In an interview, it is an automatic disqualification from the job. In a meeting, the gentleman instantly loses credibility.

2. Fit. I find this to be the most egregious mistake amongst men. Clothes that don't fit you properly are almost as bad as clothes that are not clean. If you don't know how to achieve the proper fit, you can easily go to any mall or men's store where they sell suits. They will help you determine your proper proportions, size, and fit. You can also use the subscription services mentioned above. They will take your measurements and develop full outfits for you that you can choose. Your local tailor can transform an inexpensive item

or suit into something that looks expensive based on a fit tailored to your body.

3. Shoes. Make sure that your shoes are clean, polished, and not worn looking. Again, I have seen far too many guys lose credibility because their shoes were not in good condition. This is particularly important if you're standing in front of a room full of people who can all see that your shoes are in disrepair.

4. Hair/Nails. A well-groomed hairstyle and nails are a must. The hairstyle doesn't matter so much these days as long as it's well-groomed and appropriate for the environment or setting. And, make sure your fingernails are clipped and clean.

Overall, men should have at least two to three suits that are mostly darker colors because you can wear darker colors in the winter or summer. Darker colors provide you greater flexibility and options to mix and match. Men should also have several dress shirts—at least two of which are crisp white shirts—along with the appropriate colored ties to go with the shirts. A pair of nice, polished black shoes is a must. Spending a little extra money on your shoes will ensure that they will last longer and look good for the duration. You can also take them to a shoe repair shop once a year for repairs and refreshing to keep them looking great and increase the amount of time you can keep them.

In a more casual environment, men still have to pay attention to what they wear. If your office is more relaxed, you want to make sure you have khakis, dress pants, and dark jeans. Most people go wrong in casual environments with blue jeans. You don't want to wear washed out jeans or jeans with holes/rips. Men should also avoid athletic shoes and shirts without collars, even if other people are wearing it. The goal is to be comfortable and take advantage of the casual work environment, but you don't want to be too casual because you still want to make sure that you're projecting a level of professionalism at all times.

The same is true in a very creative environment. You don't want to be the one that looks like you just rolled out of bed every day. Your clothes should still fit properly (regardless of your size), be ironed, and match. Everything should be clean and crisp no matter what type of office environment you work in or your field. It would be easy to say to use common sense, but I have seen far too often that people misstep on what many would believe to be common sense practices.

Dress for Success—Women

Women have a more complicated task for dressing in a corporate setting; they must balance looking professional with maintaining femininity and style. As a man, I admit that I have found it difficult to correct or comment on female employees' dress for this reason. Thus, I have sought out female colleagues whom I trust and whose style is undeniably appropriate and well done. Dressing for success is a necessary precursor to obtaining it. Still, many women struggle to know what is acceptable at work.

Here are Seven Key Considerations for Women:

1. Not One of the Boys. One of the common complaints from my female colleagues is having to adapt in a male dominated workforce in both performance and dress. Modern women assert that the traditions of "fitting in" with the men in the office are no longer warranted or even a good thing. Embracing your female side while being professional is key in modern day workplace as more women are in positions of power. You don't need to try to be one of the boys to be dressed well. Actually, you should look at other women who are in the roles that you desire and emulate how they show up to work.

2. Clean and Crisp. Here is an across the board goal for both men and women. Your clothes should always look clean and crisp no matter what. Invest in a great iron or a great dry cleaner and keep your clothes refreshed regularly. Beware of buying cheap clothing, cheaper fabrics, and cheap jewelry.

3. Fit. Wearing clothes that fit you properly—not too tight or too loose—affects the overall look of your outfit. Check yourself out in a long mirror before leaving the house to ensure your clothes are fitting properly.

4. The Don'ts. Avoid showing too much cleavage, or wearing midriff tops, informal clothing such as graphic T-Shirts, beach sandals, and loud "bling" jewelry.

5. Grooming. Hair should be well cut, clean, and not in extreme colors or drastic cuts. Make-up should be discreet and highlight your features. Wearing makeup has been shown to increase your chances of promotion as long as it isn't overdone.

6. Color. A color choice can make or break an outfit. In today's corporate setting, women can experiment more with colors that stand out and show your personality. Just steer clear of the neon greens and metallic fabrics that are best left for a club. Or, just left all together.

7. A Part of the Job. Understand that dressing for success is a key component to progressing and succeeding at work; take it seriously. It should be a priority if you want to succeed.

CHAPTER 6

Confidence Can Make or Break You

The confidence you project also has a significant impact on how you are received. It is also one of the characteristics that separates those who have average perceptions from those who are deemed to be exceptional. The way you carry yourself, your body language, and how organized you are is fundamental because the more confidence you express, the less others will question you. The perception is that you know what you're doing and talking about and thus, you are afforded a little more rope. You're starting from a positive brand perception instead of one from which you will have to rebound.

> "One important key to success is self-confidence. An important key to self-confidence is preparation."
>
> –Arthur Ashe

Confidence will allow you to be perceived as being:

- A better leader
- A problem solver
- Someone who gets better results (or has the ability to do so)
- A person who can handle challenges

Those perceptions turn into tangible outcomes. Confident people are promoted more often, questioned less, and generally make more money. Simply put, the silent messages you're sending when communicating with others have as much weight as what you are actually saying. For example, folded arms can mean that a person is resistant or closed, but it could also mean that the person is cold in temperature. For this reason, it is paramount to your success as an effective communicator to pay close attention to how you're showing up.

Brandon was a seasoned professional when he came to work for me. He was very smart with a great education. But he always seemed nervous and carried stacks of disorganized papers wherever he went. He hurried around like he was always late. He would come to meetings on major topics and shuffle through all of this stuff when asked a question. Again, he was competent, he had the information and the answers, but no one trusted him because they lacked confidence in his competence. It became a problem because his work was always examined under a microscope. No one wanted to sign-off on his assignments without thorough questioning because he failed to instill confidence in his peers and other managers. It became so bad that people would actually look for mistakes. He'd allowed his poorly thought out brand to become the driving narrative amongst the entire group.

On the other hand, I had a young lady on my team who was the exact opposite. She could go into meetings and get anything she asked for from any team in the organization. I decided to observe how she was showing up in these meetings that made her so effective. It was clear from the moment the meeting began that she exuded confidence. She was always prepared and her presentation was organized. Her answers to any questions were concise and when she did not know the answer she was upfront about it and promised to get an answer quickly. She walked with purpose with her head up and her shoulders back, which creates confidence in the brain and exudes confidence to others. Moreover, her presentation was in great, digestible bullet points that allowed her to present efficiently without opening herself up to greater scrutiny. The people in the room trusted her and their reaction to what she presented demonstrated it. The curious thing was that she was no more competent than Brandon; it was just how she showed up and presented herself.

Unfortunately, I had to terminate Brandon after providing coaching and giving him feedback. I implemented one-on-one preparation meetings so that he could first present to me and I could make corrections. Even still, he would come to our private meetings disorganized, so I couldn't trust him to represent our group any longer. I had lost confidence in him. His lack of confidence made other people trust him less as well, which impacted his work and ultimately impacted his job.

If your audience evaluates you as being confident and credible, you receive a positive halo making what you actually say and how you say it more credible. With that said, the positive halo is not indestructible. Again, if you are completely deficient in delivery and content, you will just as easily lose the points you won with your non-verbal presentation. Here is where the thirty-eight percent of the equation becomes important; how confident is your tone of voice when delivering the information? Based on this, your audience is either ready to receive your message or has already written you off, which is why content is only seven percent of the formula. Remember, you can have the most amazing content that will fall on deaf ears because you've failed at demonstrating credibility with the other ninety-three percent of the formula.

You have likely met people or have seen people in meetings who you wrote off as useless before they uttered a word. And then, the person ultimately won you back and blew you away. That person had to work extra hard for you to hear their message because you tuned them out and/or began to criticize their every move. You also know the opposite is true. A person comes into the room looking polished and walking with the utmost confidence for you only to discover it was all show and no substance to support the show.

A confident person is communicating that when an obstacle or challenge comes, they are going to find a solution because of the confidence they have. Thus, they are seen as someone who is better at handling challenges and is able to ascend through the ranks of the organization. It's not all show either. Your mind is a powerful machine and the things you tell yourself over and over become your reality. When you're confident in your abilities, the power of your mind allows you to find solutions when new challenges arise or when old challenges require new outcomes.

There are a few confidence-boosting tools I use and instruct my clients to use in presentations or important meetings. The power pose is one of my favorites. I have to admit that I didn't realize what it was called (or what I had been doing for so many years) until I saw a TED Talk about it. The power pose is basically a pose or stance you make that exudes power—the superman stance or similar. I usually do it in front of a mirror so that I can see it for myself.

The truth is that taking a power stance or pose affects the chemicals and hormones in the brain because you are sending positive signals that trigger confidence. I had been doing this since college, and before I knew it, it was a thing. I don't even remember what triggered me to start doing it. Before exams or big presentations, I would do my power pose in front of the mirror to get my energy going. It helps move things in a positive direction and claims a victory before I even enter the room. It is a physical manifestation of my success in communicating with others. It helps me deliver effectively in tone as well as my preparedness and organization.

Marion E. Brooks

I also use words of affirmation to build my confidence before a presentation or important interaction. I jot down these positive power words around whom I am and what I am about to do. I write things like, "You're a great presenter," or "They're going to love your presentation." I also write down the three things that I want to communicate, as well as a reminder to be confident, concise, and impactful.

Lastly, I walk with power. It is extremely important to make sure that you're walking with your head up and shoulders back when you enter and as you walk around the room (I learned this from my dad). Think of the people you see with their shoulders slumped over and head down. They are not the people you run to for advice or support. Their silent message is that they are lost or defeated. Knowing these simple things will help you build your confidence, which in turn will aid you in delivering your content in a tone and manner that makes you appear credible. The more confident you are, the more you can employ techniques like the power of pausing in your communication on certain points you want to drive home.

"Packaging plus communication skills determine whether or not others will trust you with information, give you access to decision makers, pay you a certain salary, hire you, or purchase your products and service."

–Darlene Price, President of Well Said

When communicating to a group or individual, make sure your content is clear, concise, and to the point. Sell what you need to sell and then let them ask questions for the rest of the information. Too often people information dump (show-up and throw-up), which is an ineffective way to get others to digest and comprehend your message. It also shows a lack of confidence in your understanding of the key points of communication. You have to have a strategy and structure for what you want to get across and that has to be in as few words as possible. Determine the right things to say versus everything you could say. This was something I had to learn because I wanted to make certain that people knew that I was well versed in whatever it was I was speaking about at the time. An effective communicator provides the essential, top-line information, pauses, and asks, "What questions do you have?" And if there are no questions, affirm that everyone is aligned on the information and move on to the next point.

Too many times I have seen someone talk him or herself out of a "yes" because they are data dumping information versus providing the essential information while gaining alignment. If you don't have alignment, you can have backup information to support why and how you arrived at your conclusions.

SUMMARY

1. The level of confidence you exude is directly related to the level of confidence people will have in you. People can sense timidity and fear fairly quickly.

2. Developing a confidence ritual before you enter a room will help set you up for success. Here are some quick tips that help me and many others walk into rooms ready to own it and communicate effectively.

    a. **Power Pose**. Strike a pose in the mirror that makes you feel and look powerful. Hold it for two minutes or as long as you need to change your perception of yourself. Many people strike Superman's iconic pose. I am one of those people. And it's not just for public speaking or presentations; it also works before important tests, meetings, and conference calls.

    b. **Walk with Power**. Now that you've struck your pose and held it long enough to believe it, you must walk with that power. Your head should be held up high with your shoulders back to demonstrate that you are headed in the right direction and people should follow you.

c. **Positive Self-Talk**. Words have power, especially the words we say to ourselves about ourselves. Use words of affirmation. I find that great quotes from inspirational leaders are extremely helpful (that's why I have used them throughout the book). Use them to affirm your greatness and your ability.

d. **Posture**. It's simple; sit up straight whenever you're sitting. Sitting up straight evokes power and confidence; slouching does not.

e. **Be Organized**. Besides your own appearance, the way your papers, files, and other materials look matters.

f. **Pretend**. When all else fails, there is something to be said about the adage, "fake it until you make it." All of the above takes practice and time so until you've mastered it on a conscious level keep practicing until your "pretending" becomes believing.

SECTION III—POSITIONING

POSITIONING
DEFINITION

STRATEGY THAT AIMS TO MAKE A BRAND OCCUPY A DISTINCT POSITION, RELATIVE TO COMPETING BRANDS, IN THE MIND OF THE CUSTOMER.

SOURCE: BUSINESSDICTIONARY.COM

Are you playing chess or checkers with your career? We all know that checkers and chess are two totally different games. While checkers is primarily played in the moment, chess requires a complex strategy that is often won by thinking ahead. In chess you have to plan out your strategy at least three or four moves ahead to win. Here's another difference; in checkers, each piece has an equal value and moves up the board in an "every man for himself" attempt to take out as many opponents as it can on its way to the other side. In chess, however, there is a hierarchy; the smallest piece can become queen with the right plan. It is imperative that you understand the difference in strategy for either game to have a chance at winning. When comparing checkers to chess, the primary difference is the amount of planning, strategy, and discipline required to win.

Proper career positioning includes developing a cohesive plan and strategy to achieve your goals as well as aligning with the right people. We have all heard that creating a developmental plan, networking, and having mentors are important no matter what industry you are working in. The difference is that high potentials are taught how to play chess when planning their careers, while the vast majority are left playing checkers and wondering why they are not winning.

Here are some of the benefits people with proper positioning enjoy, they:

- Are promoted more often
- Make more money
- Never feel stuck
- Have increased confidence
- Are able to work around a bad boss

Here are the three key components to effective positioning:

- Create a career or developmental plan
- Engage others in your plan—Mentors
- Continue to connect—Networking

CHAPTER 7

Understanding Your Place in the Organization

———◆—◆◆———

Understanding the structure and hierarchy of your organization is important because you need to understand the key players, the key influencers, and where you fit into it all in order to move through the matrix. Within every organization, there are those who are playing chess and are always three or four steps ahead. Then, there are the checker players who are doing their work with their head down with no foresight or planning. The checker players feel that if they continue to do a good job, someone is going to come and magically move them to the next step.

Those days are over and it's not that type of world anymore. You have to be proactive about your career and manage it. You have to position yourself effectively and strategically by connecting with the right people and demonstrating the right skill set. You have to ask for what you want. You have to tell your story, because if you don't, no one will do it for you. You have to do all these things in order to put yourself in the best position possible to reach your goals.

The bottom-line is that people hire, promote, and cast the people they know. If no one knows you, with all things being equal, the other person will get the position. It makes sense if you think about it. If you were hiring for a job and knew and trusted one of the candidates, or someone you trust recommended them, you'd be more inclined to hire that person over a stranger with a nice résumé. It isn't merely about favoritism. The person you know is less of a risk than the unknown person. Seemingly, the deck will always be stacked against a person who has few connections. If you are that person, please don't worry; I will give you some tips on how to reshuffle the deck in your favor.

I think this story will help drive home the importance of positioning. I had a guy come to me for career advice. We will call him Richard. Recently, he had been passed over for another promotion and he was very frustrated. As we talked, he explained to me that this was his fourth time applying for a promotion to director. He was a successful manager, but felt the system was rigged against him and he was at his wit's end. I asked him a few questions to get an idea of which of the four Ps was holding him back. I asked him if he knew what the common theme was for the four people who got the jobs he applied for. He said, "they already knew or had some connection to the hiring manager." Bingo! His Positioning was holding him back.

My next question was: Who is on your developmental team? Who are your mentors?

That's when he realized that it had nothing to do with his skills or performance, but everything to do with the fact that he had not aligned with the right people to demonstrate his value and skills. He was competent, but so were the people who got the jobs over him. His issue was the people who mattered didn't know him, so he was a risk when compared to the candidates they knew. We updated his developmental plan to focus on engaging mentors who could support and advocate for him when the time was right.

The Five Types of Organizational Structure[13]

It is also important to understand the type of organization in which you are working. It will have direct impact on how you position yourself and understand your current position in the organization. Henry Mintzberg is a renowned management theorist who developed a list of five basic organizational types. He identified the various organizations as a result of their blend of strategy, environmental forces, and organizational structure. The five organizational types are entrepreneurial, machine, professional, divisional, and innovative.

1. **Entrepreneurial**. An entrepreneurial company has a loose organizational structure and is typically driven by entrepreneurial-minded or creative types of leaders. Startup companies managed by their founders commonly exemplify this organizational type. Forward-thinking ideals, energy, and enthusiasm are common strengths. Limited structure, poor task discipline, inefficiency, and controlling management are potential drawbacks or risks if emphasis isn't placed on defined work processes.

2. **Machine**. Mintzberg labeled a highly bureaucratic organization as being like a "machine." Government agencies and other types of large, set-in-their-ways corporations epitomize this style. While structure, consistency, and longevity are strengths, limited openness to new perspectives and inefficiencies resulting from bureaucratic processes are common deficiencies.

3. **Professional**. The professional organization type has a similar level of bureaucracy to the machine type. However, it is characterized by a high degree of professional, competent knowledge workers who drive the economic engine. These technically skilled workers usually have specialized skills and autonomy in their work; this makes for more

13 P. Mulder (2016). *Mintzberg Managerial Roles*. Retrieved January 27, 2017 from ToolsHero: *https://www.toolshero.com/management/mintzberg-managerial-roles/*

decentralized decision-making than is prevalent in the machine type.

4. **Divisional**. A divisional structure is most common in large corporations with multiple business units and product lines. In some cases, companies divide their business and products into divisions to promote specific management of each division. Centralized control is common in this format with divisional vice presidents overseeing all facets of the work within their respective divisions.

5. **Innovative**. An organizational type that allows for cutting-edge leadership is the innovative type. This is common in new industries or with companies that want to become innovative leaders. Decentralized decision-making is a key trait as talent leaders are allowed to make judgments with efficiency in mind. The potential for leadership conflict and uncertainty over authority are drawbacks.

It is critical to your success that you determine what type of organizational structure applies because it will affect your strategies—how you play your organization's game of chess. It is equally important to understand the hierarchy and different layers, as well as what is required at each level. Then you can accurately assess how your role fits into the overarching success of the organization, which will give you a better lens to view your impact and the value you can bring to the organization as a whole. Most people think they are just doing their job while failing to appreciate the bigger picture. They should appreciate that what they are doing could affect the company overall. Effective leaders not only understand the organization's structure, but also have a keen sense of their impact on the success of the company's strategies and bottom line. When you understand the bigger picture you're able to connect things and you're able to begin to play chess. You also are able to identify ways in which you can connect with others throughout the organization in order to be even more effective and efficient while adding increased value.

For years, the term "climbing the corporate ladder" has been a widely used; I despise the term. Well, maybe not despise, but I certainly have an issue with it. When I hear climbing the corporate ladder, it sounds like someone who is trying to a get a role or job because they want a title, exposure, or the salary. Or, they want all of those things. It should be about experiences and making certain that you are aligning your skills and efforts with what the organization needs and your own personal growth/development. You want to make sure you are prepared for success in the new role you are seeking. There is nothing worse than being given an opportunity for which you are not prepared. It is a recipe for failure.

This approach and way of thinking (making sure you are prepared for success) sets you up to be personally successful and safeguards the organization's success. And, this is why it's important to understand the structure—the matrix. A role may look attractive because of the title and perks that come along with it, but it may not be right for you and thus, not a good strategy for you to seek it. By learning what it takes to be successful in the role (via mentors and sponsors) and developing your skills to match those needs, you are not climbing the corporate ladder. Instead, you're using the opportunities to grow as a professional and become a greater asset to the organization. It also develops you beyond the role and aids in your succession planning throughout your career. You take what you have learned with you wherever you go, even if you leave that company.

A perfect example was when I was offered a new role leading a marketing launch. I'd previously led two such launches successfully. I remember thinking, *what am I going to learn from this?* It was a joint venture, which was a bit different. However, I had that skill set and I knew I could do it. During that time, another mentor had recommended me for a role with a different team. In this role, I would oversee the launch of the new patient services department for the team. It was something new for me and it scared me a bit. I knew it would take me out of my comfort zone. After recognizing the skill sets, knowledge, and new exposure I would gain, I decided to take the more challenging role to continue my personal and organizational growth. In essence, it was not about climbing the ladder. It was about identifying ways and roles for me to apply my current skill set while simultaneously developing additional skills.

To that end, the best next move for you may be a lateral move. Making moves should not be focused on getting to that next level or title, but to the next level of proficiency. Prior to making any moves, you should be asking yourself key questions, such as:

1. What am I going to learn?
2. What am I going to develop?
3. What skill sets don't I have right now?
4. What experience do I need to be successful at the next level.

It is clear that you must have an understanding and strategy for moving through an organization's matrix. But I am always asked the question, how does this work for people of color (POCs) and women. Traditionally, POCs and women have had a harder time moving through the ranks of Corporate America due to archaic and patriarchal structures and blocks. It's the reality and we all know it's the reality. One of the major things that I want to impart is to ensure that you're not a victim of any situation. You have control and power over your career at all times. You may not have control or power over a particular situation or role, but you do have control over your career as a whole.

I have had a lot of clients and colleagues complain about their bosses blocking them and I know some of that is real and valid because I have seen it. My question is always, "What are you going to do about it?" At that point, you need to engage all of your tools that you've developed—your network, your mentors, and your development plan—so that you can position yourself differently. Now let's talk about how to develop those tools.

Building a Developmental Plan

Once you have properly assessed the structure of your organization, it is then time to make a plan for your career. Many people fail to plan their career so they do not have a road map to follow or benchmarks to evaluate their success. A developmental or career plan can also serve as a great tool to evaluate where you are in your career, your strengths as well as your areas of opportunity, and how all of that supports your overall objectives. Having a plan is also important because you have to make sure that in each area of your career, you have developed the requisite skill sets to be successful in the role or position in which you aspire to be.

You will build and acquire new skills more effectively if you can reference a clear professional and/or developmental plan. The clarity that a plan gives you promotes confidence when you're sharing your story with mentors, in networking situations, and while you prepare for your next level. It is why you want to make sure the plan mentions your strengths, but also your areas of opportunity that are linked to where you're trying to go and that prepare you for when you get there.

With that said, there is more than one right way to design a developmental or career plan. Some organizations have a very specific structure for employees to design and implement a developmental plan. There are also many online applications and resources that help you organize the plan. The most important thing, however, is that the plan works for you and your style. I think it is essential that you also have a plan outside of the one structured for you at your organization. Your goals and the organization's management goals for you may align in many areas, but your personal career goals should exceed those set by the organization.

The format and mechanism are up to you. There are, however, some steps and key components that I believe all career plans should have.

1. Determine your **short- and long-term objectives**. Identify what you want to do (types of roles you would like) in the short-term (six-to-twenty-four months) and long-term (three-to-six years). The goal here is to make it clear to yourself and others what you want to do in the organization. I have seen so many people frustrated because they feel stuck, but they never asked for what they want. If you want to be a supervisor, department head, CFO, or CEO, you must be clear! These short- and long-term goals are critical to developing a cohesive plan.

2. Identify **three-to-four strengths** that you currently possess that help you succeed in your current role, and will help you be successful in those prospective roles, short- and long-term.

3. Identify **two areas of opportunity**. Identify the skill sets, relationships, or experiences you need to gain in order to get to that level and be successful. For example, if you want to be a people leader and you don't have experience leading people, an opportunity could be to attain training on building and maintaining an effective culture.

4. Begin to **build the plan focused on leveraging your strengths and addressing your areas of opportunity.** The plan is the key. Leaders don't expect you to be perfect, but they do expect you to be aware of your strengths and opportunities and to have a clear plan with tangible actions to address your opportunities.

I have employed these steps many times in my career, especially when I was looking to grow or ascend to the next level within the organization and in my career. When I was transitioning into marketing, my long-term goal was to be promoted to the franchise-head level within the organization. I knew there were a couple of areas of opportunity for me to be a viable candidate for that level. I had to improve my understanding and mastery of the financial structure of the business with a focus on profit and loss management. I also needed to demonstrate that I was a strategic thinker (we discussed this earlier). Though I was fully aware that I was a strategic thinker, I still had to shift the perceptions of my professional brand within the organization.

After I identified these two areas of opportunity, I was able to focus on taking affirmative action to transform the opportunities into strengths. The first thing I did was to register for a course for non-financial managers. My next step was to secure a mentor in finance as well as work with and invest in special projects that were finance focused. Each step was written in my developmental plan with a timeline for completion attached. So, I was able to gauge where I was and make adjustments accordingly to meet the various objectives.

With regard to the strategic thinking component, in addition to the books I was reading, I also took a course that helped me to learn the language and processes that would aid in the transformation of my brand perception into one of a strategic thinker. And, of course, I started working with a mentor who was focused on strategy and operations. These were tangible things that I did to prepare for the next position and ultimately my long-term goal of being a franchise head.

After you've developed the plan, it is necessary for you to get third-party feedback from either your manager, someone above the level to which you aspire, or a mentor. You want them to look at your plan and give you feedback. Ask the following questions:

1. Do you agree that this plan will help me achieve these goals?

2. Are my strengths fully and accurately identified in the plan?

3. Are the areas of opportunity ones that will help me to achieve the goals in the plan? Are there additional areas of opportunity you see for me?

4. What are your recommendations on ways in which I can improve and strengthen the plan?

The steps to developing an effective plan are simple. The difficulty comes in the execution. The late Dr. Maya Angelou said, "Nothing will work unless you do." It is a problem faced by so many people with fitness and diet plans; they begin each year with the best plan to get in shape and eat healthy. By February, the plan has gone out of the window and they've resorted to their status quo. Don't let this be you with your career. Developing the plan and then taking affirmative action to see the plan through is what will separate you from the crowd and ensure your success.

However, as we will discuss in planning out your career, you need to be flexible and adaptable because even the best-laid plans take unexpected turns. Still, a well thought out plan will allow you to best assess whether an opportunity is aligned with your goals. It is much easier to adjust a plan than to create one during a challenge or roadblock in your career.

SUMMARY

1. Understand the structure and hierarchy of your organization to better understand your place in it.

2. People hire people they know so you have to position yourself effectively.

3. Focus your goals based on your current position and the position in which you aspire to be.

4. It's not always about getting to the next level, but about getting to the next level of proficiency, or building a new skill set.

5. Work with your manager, a mentor, and/or an executive coach, to build a developmental plan for your career.

EXERCISE

Create a developmental plan following the four steps we discussed above.

1. **Determine your short- and long-term objectives**. Identify what you want to do (types of roles you would like) in the short-term (six-to-twenty-four months) and long-term (three-to-six years). The goal here is to make it clear to yourself and others what you want to do in the organization.

2. Identify **three-to-four strengths** that you currently possess that help you now, and will help you be successful in these roles, short- and long-term.

3. Identify **two areas of opportunity**. Identify the skill sets, relationships, or experiences you need to gain to get to that level and be successful.

4. Begin to **build the plan focused on leveraging your strengths and addressing your areas of opportunity.** The plan is the key.

CHAPTER 8

Mentor Me and Sponsor My Career

❖

MENTOR
/MEN-TÔR, ˈMEN-Tәʀ/
AN EXPERIENCED AND TRUSTED ADVISER.

The next step in creating your Positioning is engaging others. I have found that all successful people have several mentors and some even have a "think tank" of advisers they enlist for different pieces of insider advice or feedback. Dr. Martin Luther King, Jr. (Benjamin Mays), Oprah Winfrey (Dr. Maya Angelou), and Barack Obama (Ted Kennedy) are a few of my favorites, but the truth is no one is going to be successful alone. Everyone needs the help of a community of people that will assist in the progression of their career.

One of my mantras is: "We are much smarter than me," so gaining perspective from people who have been there, have been successful at it, and who know the pitfalls is vital to your ability to succeed. Identifying and working with mentors is extremely important to helping to accelerate you and your career. A mentor is an individual with expertise and experience who can help develop the career of a mentee. The mentor guides, trains, advises, and promotes the career development of the mentee.

Mentors and sponsors have been just as important to my career as my education, hard work, and persistence. In fact, except for one, every new job/promotion I have received I was either hired directly by or recommended by a mentor or a sponsor. You cannot advance in your career to your fullest potential and to the level you want without great mentors. Mentors are very important because they help cultivate and develop you as a professional, and they also help identify potholes in the road before you hit them.

> "Colleagues are a wonderful thing—but mentors, that's where the real work gets done."
>
> –Junot Diaz

A mentor is someone who can help to guide you as you're doing something new or as you're engaging in a new professional activity. A great mentor has been there before and is willing to share their insights, perspectives, and support as you embark on your professional journey—whether in a specific job or lifelong professional development.

In one study of CEOs of Fortune 500 companies, eighty percent polled had mentors. They identified the following benefits:

- Access to mentors gave them insider knowledge and access to power.
- Mentoring assisted them in having careers that were fast tracked.
- It would have been much harder or even impossible to reach their current level without the support of mentors.

Mentors at work and in life are the same from a functional perspective. What they bring to the table and what you get from them mirror each other for the most part. The difference in business is that when you are developing a relationship with a mentor, some of those mentors should turn into sponsors, and there is a difference between the two. A mentor is a confidante, someone with whom you share your challenges as well as your desires. A mentor brainstorms and works with you to find solutions. A mentor helps you set goals by providing advice and information from their experiences. But you also have to do something for the mentor as well. It can't be a one-sided relationship. You have to also look to offer something of value to the mentor for the relationship to be a successful one, which may simply mean paying it forward and helping someone else.

The greatest reason why mentors are so important (and I have said this before) is that most decisions about your career are made when you're not in the room. I don't think most people understand this, which is why it is worth repeating. When they're doing your yearly evaluation, when they're determining the components of your position, and when they're deciding who will be up for the next position, you are not in the room. And that's where a mentor can transform into a sponsor and become invaluable to your success.

By developing strong relationships with key people within your organization, ones who see who you are on a daily basis, you inspire confidence in those people so that they become a sponsor. They are the ones who will start speaking for you when it matters most.

Sponsors

A sponsor is generally someone who has mentored you or for whom you have worked (many of my mentors are former bosses), but they also advocate for you when you're not present. Sponsors are willing to put their name and reputation behind you to help you move forward. They can speak to your strengths as well as your areas of opportunity, and why you are ready for advancement. You need to have an advocate who trusts that you have the skills, passion, and desire to succeed when they are in the room and you're not.

The sponsor knows who you are, what you're about, and can talk about your strengths, as well as your opportunities from a developmental perspective. A sponsor identifies to others within the organization when and why you will be a good choice for a new role and how you fit into the organization's future. I have had several great sponsors in my career. Lisa Deschamps and Kristen Harrington-Smith are both senior executives in the pharmaceutical industry. They have been two of my most active sponsors in helping guide my career. They are willing to put their reputations on the line to support me because they know I will deliver. I am grateful for and indebted to the invaluable role they have played in my professional development and career success.

With that said, not every mentor is meant to be a sponsor. You can turn a mentor into a sponsor based on your interactions with them and based on showing them your potential. For that very reason, mentoring relationships can be a double-edged sword. If you're not serious and not demonstrating competency in the mentoring relationship, it can expose you as well. You have to be invested in demonstrating growth, development, and achievement so that your mentor is willing to turn into a sponsor for you.

I have mentored people that I would not be willing to sponsor based on their lack of commitment to their own development. I will always be there to give them advice, but I am not willing to put my reputation on the line for them because they have not demonstrated that they are serious about doing the work to develop themselves.

It is important to share your goals, aspirations, and how you are growing as a professional. In order for a mentor to become an effective sponsor, they have to know your professional story—what your desires are and what you are currently working on to grow and develop. To succeed, be diligent in your interactions with your mentors. It boils down to asking the right questions. *What are your thoughts and advice? What other skills do I need to be prepared for this next role?* Then, when they see you demonstrating those qualities or working toward them while continuing to deliver at your current job, that's when they can become sponsors.

As I said before, sponsors have been invaluable for me. I did not realize at the time that most of them were mentors who would become sponsors until I reflected on my life and career. My first set of sponsors came in college after I had pledged my fraternity, Kappa Alpha Psi. As I stated in the introduction, two brothers from the alumni chapter, Michael Glover and Wallace "Blinky" Williams took me under their wings the first semester after I officially became a member of the fraternity.

I had been encouraged to run for president of the chapter even though I had only been a brother for less than a full semester. I was apprehensive because at the time I was not very comfortable speaking in front of groups. I was fine with friends and peers, but I was not comfortable in front of large groups of people (now all I need is a nice suit and a microphone and you can't shut me up).

Glover and Blinky saw something in me at that time that I guess I didn't see in myself, and they began to mentor me. They taught me everything about protocols, running meetings, and how to build my confidence in front of groups. We also worked on strategizing within and outside of the organization, and on understanding how to manage politics within the fraternity and on the campus. It was my first lesson in how to leverage and influence people. Again, the things I learned during that time are tools that I use in business today. They helped give me the confidence to eventually become the youngest president of the local alumni chapter, and to win a seat on the regional board of directors over the state of Texas.

The information and lessons that I learned in college directly prepared me for what I would later encounter with Aunt Doris. As I said, she hired me as a courier while I was in college, and when I graduated she offered me a job managing the billing and benefits department. She thought I had what it took, especially since she was so big on education and people who invested in their future. It was very interesting because I was managing people to whom I had been subordinate. As a courier, I was bringing back information from the doctors to them. Now, I was their boss. It was a very interesting transition that taught me a lot about managing people. Some were older than I and some were friends who went to high school with me, which was definitely a challenge from a leadership perspective. But one of the things Aunt Doris taught me and reinforced for me was that although I had personal relationships with my staff, it was a business and therefore it was a different playing field.

Another one of my most impactful mentors and sponsors is Reshema Kemps-Polanco. I met her during the management development program that took me from Texas to New Jersey to help train new hires. She was being promoted from her training role, so a full-time position was now open. She recommended me for her role in sales training. The challenge was I had the opportunity to become a sales manager in the Dallas area at the same time.

As I mentioned earlier, I decided to take the training role (which was a lower level promotion than a sales manager) because I knew spending time in training would make me a better manager and coach, and it afforded me more exposure and access in headquarters to mentors across various departments in the company, setting me up for longer-term success. It was one of the best decisions I have made in my entire career.

Fast forward a few years and I was doing very well as a sales manager and had been working with the marketing teams on some successful projects, but I had still not been promoted to an official role in marketing, which was my desire. I knew then that it was time for me to start crafting an exit plan so I could continue to grow.

I called Reshema (who continued to serve as my mentor) and told her that I was planning to leave. She held a high level position in the organization as only the second African American woman to be a head of marketing—a huge milestone accomplishment at the time (she is now a senior executive). Once I told her I was considering leaving, she asked me not to make a move and to give her a week. In less than a week, she called back to let me know that she had a role coming available on her team for which she felt I was a good fit. She told me to apply and that she had spoken with her vice president (VP) about me. She also told me to get my other sponsors to reach out to the VP. I interviewed with a hiring panel and then with the VP. The rest of the story is history!

Literally, at every step of my professional development and advancement, I have a story of how a mentor or sponsor helped me get to the next level of my career. Mentors who become sponsors are critical to everyone's professional development, which is why it is important to take these relationships seriously. But first, you have to find a mentor.

How to Find a Mentor

Now that it is clear how important mentors and sponsors are, let's talk about how you secure them. Many companies have formalized mentoring programs for their high potentials. A former or current boss is also a great resource for mentoring or perhaps there is someone outside of your organization who inspires you. As I mentioned previously, one of the first things I did when I became the chairman of the employee resource group was to develop a career development program. Two of my human resource colleagues and I traveled the country and spoke to employees throughout the organization about creating developmental plans, mentoring, and securing mentors, in addition to proper networking techniques. In every session, someone would say, "I'm not really comfortable seeking mentors or networking." My question when I hear that is always, "So, how's that working for you?" Granted, not everyone is a natural communicator or a people person, but at some point, it is unavoidable that you will have to develop the skills if you want to advance.

Networking—Fifteen Minutes in the Buffet Line

My fifteen minutes in the buffet line with Brian Goff turned into one of the most important fifteen minutes of my career. Brian was the vice president and head of marketing and I wanted to transition into marketing from sales. I was behind him in the buffet line at a leadership meeting and seized the opportunity to give him my elevator pitch, which landed me a time slot on his calendar.

I started by introducing myself. I explained what I had been doing in sales and my interest in moving into marketing (my elevator pitch). I asked for fifteen minutes on his calendar to gain insight from him about his career and what I would need to work on to become successful in a marketing role. Brian eventually became one of my biggest sponsors within the organization just from that one buffet line conversation. He was also one of the senior executives who encouraged me to become chairman of the employee resource group (ERG).

Networking has become somewhat of a dirty word to people because many misunderstand its purpose. For me, networking is just connecting with people. It's connecting with different people who have different experiences that you can learn from and that you can offer something to in return. Done correctly, networking is a reciprocal relationship that allows both parties to benefit. It is about identifying a happy medium or an opportunity to develop a relationship based on present or future mutual needs.

You have to network and put yourself in front of the right people if you hope to move forward within your organization and in life. It should also be noted that everyone you network or connect with doesn't have to be an executive, senior leader, or person of power. I have peers who are mentors and mentees depending on their expertise. The key is to identify and engage people who are doing or have done something you are interested in doing or learning more about.

You may not get your chance in the buffet line, but you can go through your boss or through other people who know who you are to network effectively. Request meetings with potential mentors about what they have done or are doing to see if they can become a mentor, or if they are willing, to connect you with people who can be. It is that easy. You may be thinking, *But what if they say no?* As humans, our fear of NO stops us from the YES we deserve because we don't ask. You have to push yourself outside of your comfort zone and develop the confidence that allows you to interact with people to secure these critical mentors.

The key to networking is to make sure you are authentic and don't appear as an opportunist. In addition, start networking and securing mentors before you need or want a new job. A genuine connection is what is most important.

Here is a quick story to reinforce the message. I had a job opening and a very smart, ivy-league educated young lady was recommended to me as a mentee by one of my mentors. She wanted to move into marketing from another area of the business. She was impressive, but I could not fill the position at the time. We developed a mentoring relationship, but in every meeting, she asked about open positions and was clearly not interested in getting to know me.

Eventually, she opened up and said she had received some harsh feedback through a friend that people thought she was too opportunistic and that she was turning potential hiring managers off. Truthfully, her friend was being a good friend. This young lady was identifying people with open positions and reaching out to establish a relationship. As soon as she realized that she was not getting the job or the position was already filled, she moved on from the potential relationship. She screamed opportunist, and there is nothing that is a bigger turn off than someone feeling like they are being used solely for an opportunity.

I'm not one to walk into large meetings and walk around passing out my cards hoping someone calls me. I network a little differently. I evaluate what I am trying to do or learn, and I look for people who do it well. I evaluate them, identify what I would like to learn, and then look for opportunities to connect with them with a simple, "I'm very interested in X. I know you have Y, and I want to learn more about it. Would you be willing to speak with me for fifteen minutes to share your insights?" Believe me it works because that's what I did with Brian, and I have done it regularly throughout my entire career; yet, I have been turned down only once because the person had too many mentees already. But he recommended someone else to me as a resource. People love to talk about themselves, especially when they feel that they are helping someone. I can give you a laundry list of mentors I have engaged at meetings by simply asking and connecting with them. Stop being afraid of NO and start asking for your YES!

Get Involved

Another great way to secure mentors is by joining groups and organizations that matter to you inside and outside of your company.

One of the things I wanted to do with the employee resource group to give members of the organization a platform to demonstrate their skills. Many felt that they did not have access to key decision makers in the home office, and that they were often invisible or not exposed to opportunities, especially for those in sales. I made an effort to add members of the sales force to the national board of directors for the resource group. This created an opportunity for them to meet with our advisor (who was the CFO at the time) and other members of the corporate executive committee. They all had the skills, but by being willing to join and work to help other employees, they gained the access needed to demonstrate what they brought to the table. Personally, my role as chairman helped me gain access to mentors at the next level—including the CEO and CFO of a Fortune 150 company.

Getting involved can also help you get around a bad boss. We have all experienced the person in leadership who should have never been promoted—a person who couldn't lead an ant to eat cake! It is very easy to become their victim. I have been there. However, if you take control and do your work you can effectively move around the bad boss and learn in the process.

One of my clients was having a hard time with her supervisor. She was a very talented leader (I read her reviews), but her supervisor was not supportive of her and did not give her opportunities that her peers received such as engaging with senior leadership or leveraging her talents on a national or regional level. After a few sessions, I determined that she was doing all the right things; she just needed to shift her Positioning and to get around her boss without violating protocol. She had to find another way to demonstrate her talents.

I suggested that she evaluate the employee resource groups in her organization and join one in which she was interested. Within six months, she was in a leadership role in the employee resource group and had an opportunity to present to senior leaders about a project she was leading with a community group that impacted one of the company's products. She received a nice note from one of the executives who attended the presentation. She followed up and asked him for time on his calendar to learn more about his career path and he became her mentor. Now, she was on the map! And guess what happened? Yep, her "bad boss" became a huge fan and supporter, ultimately asking her to help connect him with some of the leaders she had met. Her skills and abilities didn't change, but her Positioning did and that changed her career path.

Similar to my involvement in the employee resource group, my involvement in nonprofit organizations has also exposed me to great mentor relationships with people who have similar interests. There is an automatic commonality in nonprofits that makes it easier for you to connect. By getting involved in different organizations or affinity groups, you increase your opportunities for exposure. Even the meet-up groups within your company provide opportunities for others across the company to get to know you beyond your performance in your current role. Most major companies have groups focused on ethnicity, race, gender, military service, working parents, people with disabilities, and so on.

Also, look for volunteer opportunities in your community. Most non-profit organizations have very influential people on their board of directors. These are the business professionals who could be helpful to you and your career. You have to make sure that you're not being opportunistic; instead be genuine to your interests and who you are. Volunteer work is a great way to give back and to network.

One of the volunteer efforts that really helped me to accelerate in the eyes of some senior leadership was when I was teaching a class on proper nutrition and healthy eating to at-risk youth in Newark, New Jersey. We met on Saturday mornings through Hope International. One of my coworkers mentioned what I was doing to a senior leader who thought it was great. The senior leader asked for information on the program and the next thing I knew, I was nominated for and won our President's Award for Community Service. I wasn't doing it to impress him or anyone for that matter. I was doing it because it mattered to me. Find something that means something to you and people will take notice of your authentic commitment.

For me, getting involved in developing programs and supporting the people within the organization and community helped open up mentoring opportunities for me. It placed me on a different platform within the organization whereby people began to seek me out as their mentor, which I believe is equally important. You want to be a mentor as well. As Sunshine taught me, the more you give, the more you get. I don't do it to get something. I do it because I believe it's the right thing to do. I've always received it back two-fold because I know that when people feel the spirit in which you give, they are more willing to give to you.

Evaluate Your Current Network–Who's in Your ~~Wallet~~ Network

Another important aspect of Positioning is your overall network; the caliber of people you spend the most time with at work and outside of work. Research has shown that our annual income will be the average of the five people we spend the most time with.

Samuel L. Jackson does a great commercial for Capital One that says, "What's in your wallet." The question for me is a little different—I want to know, "Who's in your network?," because they will ultimately help determine how successful you are.

You want to align yourself with people who are now—or who are going to—where you want to go in your career. You are a reflection of the people around you, and it impacts your potential as well as your growth. The numbers and research support this as well. Thomas C. Corley conducted a research study that showed eighty-six percent of rich people (annual salary of $160K and liquid assets of $3.2M or more) make it a habit to associate with other success-minded people and limit their exposure to toxic people. On the flip side, only four percent of lower income people ($35K or less annually and liquid assets of $5K or less) in the study made an effort to associate with success-minded people.

I'm not saying you need to eradicate all of your friends. What I am saying is to ensure that you surround yourself with people who stretch you intellectually and culturally, and who have positive things going on in their lives. As they say, if you are the smartest person in your group, find a new group.

A friend told me an inspiring story about five ladies from the Cabrini Green projects in Chicago. They were all single mothers who decided they wanted better lives for their children. They felt going to college would be the best avenue. They formed a group, enrolled in the local junior college, and created a system for rotating schedules where they took turns watching the children. They all eventually graduated from the junior college, got jobs, and were able to eventually move out of the projects. That's a great example of surrounding yourself with success-minded people no matter where you are.

To that end, I was home in Texas visiting my family and someone I grew up with told me that I had "changed." He meant that in a negative way because I had turned down an invitation to go somewhere that I didn't think was wise. I didn't take offense because he was correct; I had changed. So, I said, "Thank you." The problem was he had not changed. We have to evolve or we will get left behind because someone else is always growing.

Giraffes or Turtles

In his book, *Instinct,* Bishop TD Jakes talks about the difference between giraffes and turtles. Giraffes are very tall and stately with their elongated necks and long legs, while turtles are significantly smaller and down on the ground. Turtles can't see the same things that giraffes see because a giraffe's view is much higher than that of the turtle. A giraffe lives in a different realm with a different understanding of its environment by virtue of its height and position.

Bishop Jakes' thesis is that all too often we giraffes limit the vision of our potential because of something a turtle has said to us about limitations. These negative/limiting comments create doubt and fear.

But a giraffe does not have the same limitations as a turtle, and thus can see a world that is much bigger with more opportunities than the turtle's limited view.

In planning and persisting, you have to look at the circumstances from your viewpoint. If you are a giraffe, don't allow a turtle's limited perspective to influence you. You cannot accept the turtle's story about your world because you are a giraffe. You simply can't listen to or argue with turtles. You also can't be mad at turtles because they are operating from the limited view they have, and they can't help being a turtle. It is all they know how to be.

> "You can't explain to a turtle a giraffe's decision."
>
> –Bishop T.D. Jakes

Far too often, especially in the age of social media, we get into debates with certain people who bring us down or begin to kill our confidence by poisoning what is in our psyche. The reason Bishop Jakes' analogy is so on-point is because of the size of a giraffe's heart. A giraffe's heart is huge so it can pump blood up its long neck. As such, a giraffe cannot stay bent over too long with its head below its heart or it will lose consciousness and could die. Think about when you put your head between your legs; you get dizzy quickly too. So, if a giraffe is listening to or arguing with a turtle, it has to lower itself to the turtle's level because a turtle can't rise to a giraffe's level (don't miss this analogy). Similarly, lowering yourself too long debating with a turtle could kill you and your dreams. You will kill yourself arguing with a turtle if you're a giraffe. Just keep your head up, stay focused, and don't be distracted by what the turtle is trying to tell you. You also need to surround yourself with other giraffes (this is why who's in your network is so important!).

We all need giraffes in our lives. These are people who see the best in us and push us even when we doubt ourselves. My daughter's mom Katresia is one of those giraffes in my life. If it wasn't for her, you might not be reading this book. When I started on the journey of writing the book, I was working full-time, pursuing my international certification as an executive coach, coaching clients, and launching a staffing agency. It was a lot! I decided that I would stop working on the book and focus on the other projects and priorities for a year.

When I told Katresia about my decision, she said, "Okay." Then she called me unusually early in the morning a couple of days later, I instantly thought something was wrong. She said, "I had a dream. You have to write the book this year. I don't care what else you let go. Write the book now."

She even added that our daughter Morgan could apply for student loans to finish college, if necessary, but I had to write the book now. Now that's someone who believes in you. That is what a giraffe in your life looks like.

SUMMARY

Mentoring Tips: Be Prepared

Here are a few tips provided as an overview that will ensure your mentor/mentee experiences are great ones. Set your goals and identify areas of development (career goals change).

How to Find Mentors
- Formal programs
- Corporate programs
- Business groups

- Networking!
- Internships
- Volunteering
- Supervisor

Role of the Mentee

- Establish trust and transparency
- Carefully plan and prepare meetings and other communications
- Formulate mentoring objectives and priorities
- Reflect on personal and professional strengths and areas of opportunity
- Articulate career goals and developmental needs—elevator pitch
- Create and share action plan and track progress

Role of the Mentor

- Establish trust and transparency
- Advise and provide guidance
- Help navigate through the organization (formal and informal)
- Act as sounding board for ideas
- Role model effective leadership skills and share experiences
- Advise, support, and challenge
- Coach on areas of improvement

First Mentoring Meeting

- Spend time getting acquainted

- Share a little about yourself—background, interest, hobbies, etc.

- Share past experiences and career goals

- What do you consider your greatest professional strength and area of opportunity?

- Discuss your short- and long-term professional goals

- Discuss your objective of the mentoring relationship

- Agree on frequency of meetings

Networking Tips

Here are some networking dos & don'ts:

1. Do Be Assertive, Don't Be Aggressive. You don't want to be overbearing or hover over someone.

2. Do Share Your Elevator Pitch. Introduce yourself and use your elevator pitch to engage the person.

3. Do Schedule Informational Meetings. Asking for a fifteen-to-twenty-minute call or meeting to learn more is appropriate and necessary.

4. Don't Ask for a Job. Most people will stop listening if you ask them for a job before knowing them. It's a dance that has a set order of steps.

5. Do Follow Through. If you set a meeting or get someone's contact information, be sure to follow through and follow up with him or her.

6. Do Say Thank You. A note of thanks goes a long way in this day because so many people forget to do it.

7. Do Give Back. Find ways to return the favor to those who have helped you. Networking is about relationships, and relationships are about give and take.

8. Do Use Outside Mentors. Network and seek mentors outside of your company and expertise.

EXERCISES

1. Identify one-to-three potential mentors within or outside of your organization and set up times for fifteen-minute informational meetings.
2. Find one or two organizations you can join that are within your interests.

SECTION IV—PERSISTENCE

PERSISTENCE
PERSISTENCE
PERSISTENCE
PERSISTENCE
PERSISTENCE
PERSISTENCE
PERSISTENCE
PERSISTENCE

SUCCESS

Based on the previous chapters, you have assessed your Performance (EQ), the Perceptions that affect you, and your Position within your company or profession. Now, it's time to implement. We discussed developmental plans in detail in the positioning section of the book. The processes and concepts apply for career plans, growth plans, and business plans as well. The key is when you fail to plan, you plan to fail. Eisenhower's quote means that you need to have a plan, but you also need to be flexible enough to adjust as necessary.

> ## "Plans are nothing; planning is everything."
> –Dwight D. Eisenhower

Persistence is the polar opposite of becoming a victim or giving up. No matter how well you prepare and plan, unexpected things are going to happen. Persistent people know how to take a setback and turn it into part of their setup for success. This characteristic is more important than skill, talent, or education.

CHAPTER 9

The Best Laid Plans Require Persistence

———◆———

I like to use the metaphor of a rocket to describe career planning. Rockets constantly adjust to meet their target after they launch. There is a little sensor in the nose of the rocket called the gimbal angle sensor. It evaluates the exterior environment and adjusts as necessary to keep the rocket on course. If the wind direction or speed suddenly shifts, or there are other significant changes in the environment, the sensor will adjust the trajectory and position of the rocket in order to stay on target. Be like a rocket with your career! You can't let the changes in the environment take you off track. You have to adjust to a layoff, a bad boss, getting fired, or not getting a promotion in order to stay on track for your ultimate goal.

Now, I understand that we are all human, and we have to allow ourselves space to feel disappointment, frustration, or anger. Calvin Coolidge said it this way:

> *Nothing in this world can take the place of persistence. Talent will not; nothing is more common than unsuccessful men with talent. Genius will not; unrewarded*

> *genius is almost a proverb. Education will not; the world is full of educated derelicts. Persistence and determination alone are omnipotent.*

That mind-set of taking the setback and being able to come out swinging even harder is what makes the greats great. Look at any successful person in any field in which they had to overcome obstacles and setbacks. For example, Thomas Edison reportedly failed over one thousand times before finally inventing the light bulb. There were a lot of other people trying to invent the light bulb at the same time, but he is the only one who kept going long after everyone else gave up. He was brilliant, but so were some of his peers. The difference was that he persevered in the face of his obstacles while they chose to give up.

Years ago, I heard a great sermon from a preacher in Fort Worth, Texas, entitled, "A Setback is a Setup for a Comeback." By now, most of us have heard that quote; however, that was the first time I heard it or the first time it clicked for me.

I like to think that what determines your success or failure is not the issue you're dealing with, but how you deal with the issue. Most of the challenges we face have already been faced by others. Some of those people overcame and prospered while others crashed and burned. When you have a setback, ask yourself, "Is this happening *to* me or *for* me?" Most of the time, what we perceive as a failure is actually a great lesson, or life pushing us in another (better) direction.

I read a lot of biographies and study the lives of successful people I admire. In almost every biography there is a story of the person being either fired or stopped along the way by an obstacle that seemed like a dead end. Aside from everything else she had to overcome, Oprah Winfrey was fired from a job as a news reporter. She desperately wanted to be like her idol, Barbara Walters, and had failed. Think about it, *Oprah was fired!* Instead of accepting it as full defeat, she used that moment to make an adjustment and forged her own persona and plan. Had she stayed in the moment and seen the situation as just a challenge instead of looking for an opportunity to discover her authentic calling, then she would not be where she is today. She is inarguably one of the most powerful people in the world. Think about it: Oprah Winfrey was fired from a job, and that's how she became "Oprah."

Again, having a plan, but being flexible and persistent, is paramount to successfully reaching the end goal, or at least the next goal. Oprah looked for the opportunity in what seemed like an obstacle. I often think of the millions of other potential Oprahs who gave up because of what one person did or said.

At some point we are all going to run into obstacles in our careers. It has happened to me countless times. However, those are the times to activate your network if you've done the work of building your network ahead of time. I once had a situation where I was more than qualified for a role, but they hired another, less-qualified candidate (in my opinion). At first, my ego was bruised, and I was very frustrated. It was the first time I had put my name in the hat for a job and wasn't selected. I spoke to a couple of my mentors, who all thought it wasn't the right move for me at the time, and they reminded me to be patient. Within seven months, I landed a role two levels higher than the role I originally applied for. Unfortunately, the role I originally sought was later eliminated, and the person they hired was laid off. What I thought was a disaster and an embarrassment to my brand turned out to be the best thing for me.

A family member of mine had a very successful corporate job back in the 1980s when I was growing up. She ensured that everyone knew how well she was doing. Everything was going great for her until she was overlooked for a promotion for which she felt qualified. She reacted negatively, abruptly quit her job out of anger and protest, and failed to have a well-planned strategy. She never fully recovered from her decision. Her house was foreclosed and she has spent the last few decades trying to rise back to the level of the job she quit. I often use her situation as a cautionary tale for my own career. I never leave a job without having another one or at least a well thought out plan in place. Being still in the moment and looking to respond versus immediately reacting is always the best option.

What If My Plan Is Not Working

In Chapter Seven, we talked about drafting and implementing a developmental plan. But, what if it's not working? If your developmental plan is not working, that means something isn't in alignment. Either you have a blind spot, are not putting in the requisite amount of effort, or you are misaligned with the decision makers in your organization. Now, this is not to say that your plan is going to work exactly the way you've designed it. You have to be adaptable like a rocket because outside variables will undoubtedly affect many components. But, if you're moving forward, you will definitely be in a better place to succeed with a tangible plan.

I always think of someone sitting on the shore of a body of water while debating with themselves as to which way the tide will take them when they climb into the boat. Meanwhile, another person is already *in* the boat even though it might take different turns. But guess what? They're moving forward inside the boat while the other person is stuck in the status quo. Your plan might turn right or it might turn left, but having a plan and acting on it will allow you to move toward your ultimate objective.

> Fears are emotions; they are not real. You can walk through them if you make up your mind to take the first step and keep going...
>
> –Magic Johnson

We have to get in the boat and keep going; and we do not give up until we reach our goal! The issue I see is that so many people are afraid to start (get in the boat) because they don't have a guarantee of how it's going to end.

Optimism and Persistence

Optimism fuels innovation. It helps keep you focused on being solution oriented, and it helps shift you from the setback mind-set to a comeback mind-set by focusing on the solutions and lessons learned versus seeing the challenge as insurmountable.

Persistence is a state of mind that directly reflects what you believe about yourself. If you believe that you are destined and deserving of success, then you don't take no for an answer—at least not a final answer. Successful people use optimistic language like, "I can" or "I have" or "I will." They have an optimistic mind-set where they believe good things are permanent and bad things are temporary—or at least they are a learning opportunity. So, the optimist works even harder to find a solution to overcome setbacks.

Alternatively, a pessimistic mind-set believes that bad things are permanent and good things are temporary. I have noticed that many people who don't succeed in meeting their goals have become victims of their own lives. They've given their power away and have allowed other people and external circumstances to derail their plan and, therefore, their progress. It then becomes about how someone else's actions have prevented them from moving forward when they, in fact, are in absolute control. As long as we continue to push forward and learn, every obstacle that we face becomes an opportunity on our pathway to our goals (in a free society).

A study was conducted on fifteen thousand MetLife sales agents to determine the impact of optimism on their performance. The agents who scored in the top fifty percent in optimism sold thirty-seven percent more insurance than those who scored in the bottom fifty percent. And those who scored in the top ten percent in optimism sold eighty-eight percent more insurance than those who scored in the bottom ten percent in optimism. The study showed that optimism was a better indicator than traditional hiring assessments in determining success.

It's important to discuss what happens when we encounter obstacles and how to change the way we react to them. The challenge is not the "thing," it's how you respond to the "thing," that will make or break you. I coach my clients to first slow down and evaluate the facts of the situation, not the emotions surrounding the situation. Just the facts. The great majority of situations, when considered solely on the facts, are much less daunting than the emotional baggage we attach to them.

You have to give yourself time to deal with the shock of the situation. However, if you change the way you look at the situation, a challenge can become an opportunity. The opportunity won't show itself if you're complaining about it, which keeps you in the same moment. Instead, take time to pause and look for the lesson, which allows you to keep learning, growing, and ultimately moving forward. As you continue to expand, you become a lot more resilient every time you stand back up after being knocked down.

One naturally human response is to put ourselves down or complain about what someone else did to us. Instead, picture how that person looks for a moment with their head down and their shoulders slumped over. I tell people to stop, lift up your head, and ask yourself what's the opportunity here? How can I use this situation in the future to help someone else or myself? The options will start to appear (prefrontal has been activated), and now you are preparing for success.

Serena Williams is the epitome of persistence and employing an optimistic mind-set, in her matches and in her career. She is one of those rare athletes who is able to be down in the count and still find a way to win. The truth is that while her athletic ability and training may be rare, her persistence has been learned and perfected with practice. We all have that power to keep going and to choose the conversation within ourselves that transforms the trial into triumph. The truth is, the more you do it for yourself, the better equipped you are to do it for other people. This is the characteristic that makes for an ideal manager or executive. Hope and optimism give the space to develop a strategic plan. Serena *always* believes she will win, which is one reason she does.

> I never lose, I either win or learn.
>
> —Nelson Mandela

When you have an optimistic and persistent mind-set you are willing to put in the work. You never truly fail because you are always learning and moving forward.

Expectations (mind-set) drive behaviors and behaviors drive outcomes. For example, in a study of thirteen people who were highly allergic to poison ivy, researchers told them that the poison ivy was a regular leaf and that the regular leaf was poison ivy. They were asked to rub the regular leaf, which they thought was poison ivy, on one arm, and the actual poison ivy on the other arm. Only two of the thirteen participants broke out on the arm rubbed with poison ivy. All thirteen broke out on the arm rubbed by the placebo leaf. What the mind expects, it usually receives. Expect positive things and they are drawn to you.

The Bad Boss (Revisited)

More than likely, you've had a bad boss. I think the overwhelming majority of people in the workforce have had at least one bad boss for a variety of reasons. A bad boss can also be an opportunity if you can find a pathway around them, but you have to have the right lens.

I once had a manager whom I considered a "bad boss." I mean he drove me nuts. He was a micromanager and everyone on the team was super frustrated with him and his leadership style. We complained to each other a lot. One week we were superstars if the trend line looked good. The next week he wanted an action plan on how we were going to fix the territory. Then, the next week we were stars again. He was a nice guy, but he had no business leading people.

Okay—I have to admit it—I was playing the victim. I finally realized that I was contributing to my own misery by constantly focusing on how much I hated his management style. At the time, I was not leading people, but it was clearly part of my developmental plan. So, I shifted my focus to evaluating him like a case study of what *not to do* when I led my own team again. That shift in perspective changed everything for me. In the end, I learned as much from him as I did my good managers about how to lead a team and build an effective culture.

I told you the story about my client who worked around a bad boss by joining an employee resource group that led to her securing a senior leader as a mentor. She did it the right way. The wrong approach would have been for her to go around the organization bashing her boss. She also would have broken protocol by interviewing for roles without telling her current boss. That is considered career suicide within most organizations.

Other managers are always going to tell your boss that you're interviewing for other roles, even if it's merely for feedback on your performance and personality. Your boss will find out, so you must inform them if you're applying for another role within the organization. A better approach is to do what she did. You can reach out to people for mentoring. You can network. Or, you can join a group or organization that will allow you to do some work and gain connections that are beyond your boss without stepping on your boss' toes.

Activate Your Network

Life is not always so simple and easy, and this can cause skepticism. My goal is not to discount the reality that life will present challenges, which can be extremely difficult. We do reach dead ends in some situations. Yet, there is still an opportunity. Actually, I believe there are no real dead ends in life as long as you are breathing. If you have done the first three Ps and you are persistent, you will always find opportunities. They might not look like what you thought, but you will find success.

After you've done all of this work and are still not getting anywhere, it's easy to feel frustrated and defeated. If you allow yourself to stay caught in the situation versus owning your power, you will get stuck. I had a coaching client hit what she perceived to be a dead end at her job after she'd successfully implemented all the practices that we have discussed in this book. Naturally, she felt frustrated and defeated until I encouraged her not to assume the victim role, but rather think about what she could do to change her situation.

All of the work we'd been doing kicked in and she concluded, "I need to activate my network." *Exactly.* It was time for her to reach out to all the people who were sponsors, mentors, and allies within her network in order to find another opportunity outside of her current organization. It was time to move on. Knowing when it's time to make an exit is equally pivotal in continuing the plan on your pathway toward your goal. Persistence does not mean ignoring the realities that are simply not working and still stay in the situation. It means to not let a failed situation, or one that is destined for failure, stop you.

Recently, a colleague was told that he was not qualified for a director-level position in the organization for the second time. He activated his network and went to the number one company in the industry as a director. But wait, it gets better; within eight months of going to the new organization, he was promoted again.

It would have been easy for him to sit and complain about how unfair and wrong they were about him, but he took action because he had done his work. His adversity opened up a new opportunity that led to something much bigger than what he thought was possible a few months prior. As Milton Berle said, "If opportunity doesn't knock, build a door!"

One of my favorite movies, *The Pursuit of Happyness* starring Will Smith, is a great illustration about how someone else's viewpoint can influence your perceptions, but should not. Will Smith plays Chris Gardner (on whose real life the film is based) who essentially hits rock bottom. Chris is playing basketball with his son and his son tells him that he is going to be a professional basketball player. Chris tells him that it's not a realistic goal because he will likely be as good as he was, which means he won't make it to the professional league. After which, his son throws the ball and says he doesn't want to play basketball anymore.

Chris catches himself and displays excellent emotional intelligence. He sees what he has just done to his son and says, to paraphrase, "You know what son? Don't let anybody limit your dreams or what's possible for you just because they couldn't do it or can't see it. You need to make sure that you go out there anyway, and if you want to do it, go get it."

I think that's such a powerful scene and message. It is also related to the giraffe and turtle story. Oftentimes persistence is ensuring that the messages you consume are consistent with your goals and not poisonous derailers that prevent forward motion. The limitations someone else tries to place on your life are derived solely from what they believe and are not your truth.

Here is another real-life example. I had a client in the beauty industry. She was in the hospital and a family member sent messages to clients canceling appointments and letting them know there was a family emergency and that she would be out of work for at least a week. A few of her clients were angry and aggressive (the vast majority were kind and concerned) when she returned and it hurt her feelings. It also stressed her out at a time when she clearly did not need the additional stress. Based on those individuals, she decided to take a hiatus from her business largely due to her frustration with the negative people. We worked on not letting "people who don't matter too much matter too much."

> ## "Don't let people who don't matter too much matter too much."
>
> –Wes Moore

First, we did what is known as a 10-10-10 to reframe the conversation and the importance of the negative feedback on her reputation (that was her concern). The 10-10-10 is another coaching tool I use to help people get unstuck in the micro and to help them see the broader picture. It was developed by Suzy Welch to help keep the situation in perspective.

1. How will I feel about this in ten minutes?
2. How will I feel about this in ten months?
3. How will I feel about this in ten years?

The 10-10-10 helps reframe the situation in your brain from a distance so that you see things more clearly. It allows you to focus on the facts versus emotions. My client and I looked at the facts: 1) She was in the hospital, and 2) There wasn't anything she could have done differently. She certainly wasn't going to run out of the hospital in a hospital gown because a client wanted her hair done. Absurd.

Next, we practiced what to say to herself when engaging with negative clients: *Don't Let People Who Don't Matter Too Much Matter Too Much*. We worked on changing the questions she asked herself during the interactions. *How do I maintain leadership in this conversation? How do I state the facts in a loving and kind way?* For example, "I was in the hospital and apologize for missing your appointment. Here are your options. Please let me know how you would like to proceed." Then, I reminded her not to take any of it personally. Her clients' reactions were about them and not about her being in the hospital. The plain and simple fact is that those who are unhappy don't want you to be happy. You always have the option to either let them dictate your mood and behavior or to control the situation. My client said it worked and she was able to look at their anger as their problem and not take it personally. She stayed separated from their drama and ultimately controlled the situation, but more importantly she controlled her emotional response.

Persistence Personified

I mentioned Thomas Edison earlier; he is one of my favorite historical figures and examples of persistence. Thomas Edison became one of the most famous and essential inventors in the history of the world. Partly due to his poor upbringing and limited resources, Edison was considered insignificant. No one believed that he was going to ever amount to anything (sound familiar). They certainly didn't think he was ever going to successfully harness electricity. His failures were legendary in his time. Thomas Edison, himself, is legendary because he never allowed his background or those failures to stop him from reaching his goals. Each time he failed, he looked at it as an opportunity to learn and do it better the next time. Thomas Edison's persistence led to more than one thousand patents, including the phonograph, the motion picture camera, and the electric light bulb. *It's not where you grow up; it's what grows up in you!*

Tina Turner exhibits another admirable example of persistence. I think we all know the story of her poor upbringing and violent marriage (and successful career) with her ex-husband Ike Turner. There is a famous scene in the movie, *What's Love Got to Do with It* where Angela Bassett as Tina Turner is in divorce court in 1976 and decides to give him everything she had worked so hard for and endured so much to have. She gave him the royalties to all the music, the cars, and the houses. Everything! It was as dramatic moment. When I saw it in the theater, the crowd roared and clapped for her. What most people don't know is she was flat broke for years, was on food stamps, and she started cleaning other people's houses at one point to make ends meet. Add to it that her first two solo albums were commercial failures.

For most people, that would have been the end of their story, but not for Tina Turner. She continued to work hard on her music, aligned herself with great supporters and mentors like Ann Margret and Roger Davies, and in 1984 she successfully launched a huge comeback. Tina Turner has been ten times more successful in her solo career than she was with Ike. She also holds the Guinness World Record for most concert tickets sold in addition to a slew of GRAMMYs and other honors. Most people would have thought their best days were behind them after the divorce and challenges she faced, but she persevered. Look at the outcome.

Those are two examples of legends. I share those because I want you to know that they were not always legends. Instead of giving up when the odds were stacked against them, they persevered, which is what made them legends. Their stories also reinforce that success isn't a passive sport. You have to work hard and be persistent. I sacrificed a lot of time, money, and energy to succeed to the point where I am today. I worked at night, on weekends, and skipped vacations to attain my international certification as an executive coach, start my own business, and write this book. As I said previously, I read at least fifteen books a year so I can stay fresh and insightful in order to be the best resource to my clients. It would have been much easier to party and vacation after work. Now, I still have a full, happy life, but when it's time to focus, I sacrifice immediate gratification for my long-term success. As Iyanla Vanzant says, "You have to do your work." It's true, if you want success, you have to put in the time and work…and remain persistent. I recently saw a great quote online that crystallizes this point, *"If you want to be part of the 1%, you have to do what the other 99% of people are not willing to do!"*

That is the consistent theme with these examples. They each put in the work, even when it didn't look like it was going to come to fruition. Thomas Edison and Tina Turner believed in what they were doing so much that they continued to work toward their dreams even while others were laughing at them. As amazing as all of the famous people I have mentioned in this book are, they are not super-human—they just applied lessons that they learned along the way to plan for success.

I do not claim to have outlined all the tools that lead to a successful career and life in these pages: however, I do believe that I have provided a framework to take your career by the horns and steer it in the direction of your dreams. You are no different than Edison, Tina, Serena or Oprah—you're made of the same stuff they are. It's what you do with that stuff and the things you've learned in this book (and beyond) that make the ultimate difference. If a poor African American boy from Fort Worth, Texas, who was discounted and counted out from day one can achieve the level of success I now enjoy, you can do it too.

I've given you access to the information and the tools that are proven to help you and your career. I believe that just by reading this book, you have jumped ahead of half of the people who don't know what they don't know. You're on your way to the success you have dreamed of and deserve. Now, go out there, and like Nike's slogan says, "Just Do It."

MARION E. BROOKS
EXECUTIVE COACHING

Marion is a sought-after trainer, keynote speaker, and career and personal coach. If you or your organization would like a deeper dive into the 4 Keys that were discussed in this book, Marion offers customized one-on-one coaching, group workshops, and keynote presentations that will help transform your career, your team/group or organization. For more insight and inspiration, you can contact him at www.MarionEbrooks.com and MBrooks@marionEbrooks.com.

Social Media
Facebook: Facebook.com/MarionEBrooksPPD
Instagram/Twitter: @MarionEBrooks